The Woman in White

WILKIE COLLINS

Level 6

Retold by Anne Collins
Series Editors: Andy Hopkins and Jocelyn Potter

Pearson Education Limited
Edinburgh Gate, Harlow,
Essex CM20 2JE, England
and Associated Companies throughout the world.

ISBN: 978-1-4058-8276-7

First published in 1859–60
Published in the Penguin English Library 1974
Reprinted in Penguin Classics 1985
New edition first published 1999
This edition first published 2008

9 10

Typeset by Graphicraft Ltd, Hong Kong
Set in 11/14pt Bembo
Printed in China
SWTC/09

Penguin Books Ltd a Penguin Random House Company

For a complete list of the titles available in the Penguin Readers series please write to your local
Pearson Longman office or to: Penguin Readers Marketing Department, Pearson Education,
Edinburgh Gate, Harlow, Essex CM20 2JE, England.

Contents

Introduction

There, in the middle of the wide road — there, as if she had just that moment sprung out of the earth or dropped from heaven — stood the figure of a lonely woman, dressed from head to foot all in white.

'Is this the road to London?' she asked.

The Woman in White takes place in mid-nineteenth century England. On the last night before he travels to the north of England, Walter Hartright, a young art teacher, meets a young woman dressed all in white. She seems lonely and frightened and Walter helps her find her way to London. As the two talk, Walter learns something very strange, something that signals the beginning of a dramatic change in the young man's life.

Two days later, Walter starts his new job at Limmeridge House, teaching art to two half-sisters, Marian Halcombe and and Laura Fairlie. The girls' parents are dead, and they are now under the protection of their uncle, Mr Frederick Fairlie. Walter immediately becomes good friends with the older sister Marian, who is lively and intelligent, but it is the beautiful, fair-haired Laura whom he falls in love with. However, one thing immediately puzzles him: why does Laura look so much like the Woman in White?

For many months, Walter and the two sisters work happily together. Then Walter learns that Laura promised her dead father that she would marry a man called Sir Percival Glyde and that he will arrive in a few days. Just before he does so, Laura receives a note warning her that Sir Percival is an evil man and that if she marries him, she will be in danger. It soon becomes clear that Sir Percival is interested in the large amount of money that Laura will receive on her twenty-first birthday. But can selfish Mr Fairlie be persuaded to object to the marriage settlement that Sir Percival insists on? And if the marriage takes place, can Marian and Walter rescue Laura from Sir Percival and his brilliant, evil friend, Count Fosco?

Finally, what is the dangerous secret that the Woman in White (whose real name is Anne Catherick) knows about Sir Percival? Could her life be in danger too? And what is the connection between her cold, hard mother, Mrs Catherick, and Sir Percival?

These are some of the mysteries that Walter and Marian struggle to solve and that make *The Woman in White* so exciting to read.

Wilkie (William) Collins, the son of a landscape painter, was born in London in 1824. He was educated privately but considered that his real education was acquired during trips around Europe with his family. He discovered his gift for storytelling while he was still a schoolboy. As a young adult, he worked for a tea importer for a few years and then studied law. However, he soon realized that his real love was writing. He wrote a book about his father, which was published in 1848, and a historical novel called *Antonina or the Fall of Rome* (1850).

Collins traveled a lot, spending time in France, Italy and the United States, often with his friend, the great writer Charles Dickens, whom he met in 1851, and who had a great influence on him. He worked with Dickens on theatrical and writing projects and wrote many articles and short stories for his magazines. The two remained good friends until Dickens's death.

Collins wrote articles, short stories and plays, but his real talent was for writing novels. He wrote several during the 1850s, the best of which was *Basil* (1852), an exciting mystery story. However, it was in the 1860s that Collins wrote his most famous mystery novels, and these made him one of the most popular writers of the time and remain popular today. These were *The Woman in White* (1860) and *The Moonstone* (1868). Other novels of this period include *No Name* (1862) and *Armadale* (1866).

The novels that Collins wrote after 1870 were less successful, although his books still sold well. He was repeatedly ill during this period, and he also appeared to be more concerned with social issues, such as divorce, than with the quality of his stories. His private life was very unusual for those times; he lived for years with a woman called Caroline Graves, and at the same time kept Martha Rudd, the mother of his three children, in a second home. He did not marry either of them.

Collins died in 1889. Before his death he gave instructions for the words that he wanted on his gravestone: his full name, dates of birth and death, followed by the words 'Author of *The Woman in White* and other works'. Like many of his readers, Collins regarded *The Woman in White* as his best novel, better even than his other great mystery novel, *The Moonstone*, also in Penguin Readers.

Collins' importance in English literature comes not only from the quality of his work but also from its originality. His stories were the first full-length detective stories in English. His plots were brilliantly constructed, and the writer T. S. Eliot called *The Moonstone* 'the first, the longest and the best of modern English detective novels'. Collins used three kinds of detectives in his books: ordinary people (like Walter and Marian in *The Woman in White*), professional police detectives (Sergeant Cuff in *The Moonstone*, for example), and extremely unpleasant private investigators (like James Bashwood in *Armadale*).

These works sold widely in Britain, the United States and Europe, and were translated into many other languages. Collins's own advice to other writers was: 'Make 'em laugh, make 'em cry, make 'em wait.'

In the mid-nineteenth century when *The Woman in White* was written, Britain was experiencing great social change as a result of the Industrial Revolution. The development of factories meant that huge numbers of people moved from the countryside to the new industrial cities. These changes accelerated the growth of the middle classes, but the upper classes were still very powerful, often abusing their privileges, and there was a very big gap between them and the poor.

In *The Woman in White*, the upper-class Sir Percival Glyde is shown to be a truly evil man. It was common in nineteenth century novels for an upper-class man to marry a wealthy woman in order to clear his debts, as Sir Percival aims to do. But Sir Percival and his equally wicked friend, Count Fosco, are also prepared to commit crimes to maintain their wealth.

Women in the mid-nineteenth century had much less freedom than men. In the novel, Laura, as the daughter of an upper-class family, is expected to marry a man who will improve her family's position in society. It was also customary for the husband to benefit from a marriage settlement in which he received money from his wife's family. Women without an inheritance were in a weak position, as Marian is, depending on marrying well in order to improve the quality of their lives. Life for women of the servant class, to which Anne Catherick belongs, could be much more difficult, and they were always at the risk of abuse by their employers.

The Woman in White first appeared in parts between 1859 and 1860 in the popular magazine *All The Year Round*, started by Charles Dickens. The novel was so successful that every week there were long queues of people waiting to buy the next issue of the magazine. The idea for the character of the Woman in White came from Collins's first meeting with a mysterious lady, dressed all in white, one evening in London. The author and a friend, the English painter John Millais, were out walking when they heard someone scream. A beautiful young woman then came running towards them, asking for help. Collins followed her and did not return. The lady was Caroline Graves, who later lived with him.

The story in the novel may seem improbable, but we now know that Collins based it on a real French court case which was described in a book he bought from a bookstall in Paris. The main characters in the novel even look like the people in the court case!

Although T. S. Eliot described *The Moonstone* as the first full-length English detective story, many people consider that the *The Woman in White* was really the first. Although there are no actual detectives in the story, Walter and Marian act just like detectives as they struggle to discover Sir Percival's secret and save Laura from him.

Plot is of central importance to this type of story, and the plot of *The Woman in White* is clever and complex. Some of the characters, however, do not create the same level of interest: Laura is a typical romantic heroine, and Sir Percival is a typical bad character; neither of them have any depth of character. On the other hand, Count Fosco is an interesting, very unusual character, and Marian is a positive and very powerful female heroine.

In the novel, Collins experiments with an unusual way of telling a story: the story is told from the point of view of a number of different characters, adding greatly to the interest of the novel.

Collins's great skill as a storyteller means that today's reader will enjoy *The Woman in White* just as much as readers did when the novel first appeared.

PART ONE

The story is told by Walter Hartright, teacher of art

Chapter 1 The Woman in White

It was the last day of July, 1849, and the heat in London had been terrible all day. I was sitting in my room, trying to read, but I couldn't concentrate on my book. It was too hot and the constant noises from the street disturbed me. So as I had many things to think about, I decided to go for a walk in the cool evening air.

My name is Walter Hartright and I'm an art teacher. This was my last night in London. Early the following morning I was due to travel to Cumberland in the north of England. I had been offered a job there – at a place called Limmeridge House, near the small village of Limmeridge.

My future employer was a gentleman called Mr Frederick Fairlie. He had advertised for an art teacher to teach drawing and sketching to his two nieces. This teacher would live at Limmeridge House with the family.

I knew I was very lucky to get this job. Teaching the young ladies would be easy and pleasant, and the pay and working conditions were excellent. But at the same time I had a very strange feeling about the job. I didn't want to take it, but I couldn't explain why. Perhaps even then I knew deep inside that it would change my life for ever.

I was still thinking about Limmeridge House when I reached Hampstead Heath, a wide area of open parkland in the north of London. By now the moon had risen and the night air felt wonderful – fresh and cool.

There was a road stretching out across the Heath and I began to walk along it. Nobody else was around. I was passing by some trees on one side of the road when suddenly somebody touched me lightly on the shoulder from behind.

Every drop of blood inside me froze. I turned round, my hand tightening on the handle of my stick.

There, in the middle of the wide road – there, as if she had just that moment sprung out of the earth or dropped from heaven – stood the figure of a lonely woman, dressed from head to foot all in white.

'Is this the road to London?' she asked.

Her face looked thin and pale in the moonlight, and there was something very sad about her expression. She had fair hair and large trusting eyes, and in her hand she carried a small bag. I guessed her to be about twenty-two years old.

What on earth was such a woman doing all by herself in this lonely place?

'Please, sir,' she repeated, 'is this the road to London?'

'Yes,' I replied. 'But where did you come from? I didn't see you until you touched me. You gave me quite a shock.'

'I was hiding among those trees,' she replied. 'I saw you pass by, but I was afraid to speak to you until I had seen your face. When I saw that your face was kind, I followed you and touched you. Will you help me?'

She looked so sad and lonely that I agreed. I couldn't do anything else.

'All right,' I said. 'Tell me how I can help you.'

'I don't know London very well,' she said. 'But I have a friend here, a lady, who will be very glad to see me. I can stay with her but I need to carriage to take me to her house. Can you help me find one?'

'Yes, of course,' I said. 'Come with me.'

We set off walking back to London together. The whole

There, in the middle of the wide road — there, as if she had just that moment sprung out of the earth or dropped from heaven — stood the figure of a lonely woman, dressed from head to foot all in white.

experience was like a dream. Who was this mysterious woman?

'I want to ask you something,' she said suddenly. 'Do you know anybody in London with the title of Baronet★?'

As she asked me this, she was staring hard into my face. I was astonished by her question.

'Why do you ask?' I said.

'Because there is one baronet who is cruel and wicked,' she replied. 'I hope you don't know *him*.'

'No,' I said, I don't know any baronets. I'm only a humble teacher of art. Who is this wicked baronet?'

'I can't tell you any more,' the woman said, looking very upset. 'Please don't ask me any more questions.'

We walked for some time in silence before she spoke again.

'Do you live in London?' she asked.

'Yes,' I replied. 'But tomorrow I'm going away to the north of England – to Cumberland.'

'Cumberland!' she repeated. 'How I wish I was going there too. I was happy in Cumberland once. When I was a child, I spent several months in a village called Limmeridge and I went to the local village school. It was run by a dear, kind lady called Mrs Fairlie, who was my good friend. Mrs Fairlie's husband was very rich and they lived in a big house, called Limmeridge House, just outside the village.'

Now it was my turn to stare. Limmeridge House was the very place I was going to. I couldn't believe it.

'Mrs Fairlie is dead now,' continued the strange woman. 'She had a pretty little girl a bit younger than I was. I suppose the little girl must have grown up and gone away.'

I was about to ask my mysterious companion some more questions, but by now we were getting near the centre of

★ *Baronet: a man from a noble family, who holds a high position in society*

4

London. As we turned a corner, we noticed a carriage standing outside some houses.

'I'm so tired,' said the woman. 'I don't think I can walk any further. Let me take that carriage.'

I saw that the driver had a kind face and I was sure he wouldn't harm her. She got into the carriage but I didn't hear what address she gave to the driver. The carriage set off slowly. Gradually the sound of its wheels grew fainter as it disappeared into the darkness.

The Woman in White had gone.

Chapter 2 Walter Arrives at Limmeridge House

The following day I travelled to Cumberland. The journey was very long and it was late in the evening when I arrived at Limmeridge House. Except for one servant, everybody had gone to bed, and as I was very tired, I went to bed too.

Next morning, when I got up, the sun was shining. From my window I had a wonderful view of the gardens stretching down to the bright blue sea in the distance. It was all so different from my tiny room in London that I began to feel enthusiastic and happy about starting my new life.

At nine o'clock I went downstairs to the breakfast room. When I opened the door, I saw a young lady standing by the far window, looking out across the garden. She turned and came towards me, holding out her hand and smiling warmly.

She had thick black hair and dark shining eyes. She wasn't at all beautiful but the expression on her face was bright, friendly and intelligent. I liked her immediately.

'Good morning, Mr Hartright,' she said. 'I hope you slept well. I'm Marian Halcombe, one of your two pupils here. Laura, your other pupil, is still in her room. She has a slight headache, but

5

you'll be able to meet her later.'

'Is Laura your sister?' I asked.

'She's my half-sister,' replied Miss Halcombe. 'My mother married twice. Her first husband was Mr Halcombe, my father. Then he died and later my mother married Mr Fairlie, Laura's father and the owner of Limmeridge House.

'Although we shared the same mother, Laura and I are very different both in character and situation. My father was poor and Laura's father was rich, so I have no money and she has a fortune. I'm ugly and bad-tempered and she's beautiful and behaves like an angel.'

'Is Laura's father dead too?' I asked.

'Yes. His brother, Mr Frederick Fairlie, your employer, is now the owner of this house. You'll meet him after breakfast. He's not very keen on visitors; he has great trouble with his nerves and never leaves his room.

'I do hope you'll be happy with us,' continued Miss Halcombe. 'We enjoy living here, but it's very quiet. We don't have any of the excitement or adventures which you must be used to in London.'

Immediately her words reminded me of the Woman in White.

'I don't need any more adventures,' I said. 'Two nights ago, I had an adventure which I will never forget.'

Then I told Miss Halcombe about my meeting with the mysterious woman on Hampstead Heath.

'The strange thing is that she mentioned your mother, Mrs Fairlie,' I said. 'She seemed to have known her and loved her very much. Do you know who this woman can possibly be?'

Miss Halcombe shook her head. She looked interested but also astonished. Clearly she had no idea who the Woman in White could be.

'It's a complete mystery,' she said. 'But I have an idea which may help us to solve it. Upstairs I have a large collection of my mother's letters. I'll read through them and see if I can find any information about this woman. Meanwhile, it's time for you to visit Mr Fairlie.'

We arranged to meet later and I went upstairs to Mr Fairlie's room. He was sitting in an armchair, reading. He was about sixty years old with a delicate, nervous face. When he spoke, his voice sounded tired and complaining. As I came into the room, he waved his hand towards a chair.

'Do sit down, Mr Hartright,' he said. 'But would you mind not making any noise. My nerves are very delicate, you know. Have you got everything you want? Do you like your room?'

'Everything is fine,' I started to say, but to my surprise Mr Fairlie held up his hand and stopped me.

'Please,' he said, 'would you mind not speaking so loud? My nerves are very delicate. Have you met Marian and Laura?'

'I've only met Marian,' I said. 'What kind of art would you like me to teach the two young ladies?'

'I'm afraid I don't feel strong enough to discuss that,' said Mr Fairlie. 'You must ask Marian and Laura. Mr Hartright, it's been a great pleasure meeting you, but now I'm getting tired. Please excuse me, and please don't bang the door on your way out. So kind of you. Good morning!'

It was a great relief to get out of Mr Fairlie's room. Clearly he was a very self-centred person who was interested in nothing except his own health. I went downstairs and found Miss Halcombe waiting for me.

'Laura's in the garden,' she said. 'Do come and meet her.'

On the way she said, 'I've found out something interesting. I've been reading my mother's letters and in one of them she mentions a little girl called Anne Catherick, who was visiting Limmeridge one summer with her mother. My mother had set up a school for the village children and while Anne was in Limmeridge, she went to this school.

7

'My mother writes about Anne Catherick with great affection. Anne told her that she would always wear white to remember her by, as my mother's favourite colour was white.'

'So it's quite possible that the Woman in White is Anne Catherick grown-up,' I said slowly. 'What happened to Anne?'

'I don't know,' said Miss Halcombe. 'She and her mother left Limmeridge after a few months and never came back. There is no further mention of her in my mother's letters.'

As we were talking, we had been walking across the garden to the summer house. I saw a young lady sitting inside at a table, drawing, with her head bent closely over her work. She was wearing a pretty summer dress and had golden hair.

'There's Laura,' whispered Miss Halcombe. Then more loudly she said, 'Laura, I've brought our new art teacher, Mr Hartright, to meet you.'

At once the young lady looked up from her drawing and her eyes met mine. She had a lovely face and the most beautiful smile in the world. But there was something else about her too – something that troubled and disturbed me. Had I met her before? I didn't think so. But she reminded me of somebody I knew.

Then I realized. Impossible as it may seem, Laura Fairlie looked very much like the Woman in White!

Chapter 3 Laura Receives a Warning

During the following months, I experienced some of the happiest and most peaceful moments in my life.

Every afternoon I went with Miss Halcombe, or Marian as I'll now call her, and Laura into the countryside to draw and paint. I enjoyed Marian's company very much and I admired and respected her greatly. But feelings of a different kind were awakening within me for Laura.

Every day Laura and I were growing closer. As I was teaching her how to hold her pencil to draw, my hand would nearly touch her hand or my cheek would touch her cheek. At those moments, I could smell the sweet perfume of her hair.

In the evenings after dinner we would light the tall candles in the sitting room and Laura would play the piano. She played with great feeling and I loved to sit and listen to the beautiful music while darkness fell outside.

The truth was that I was falling deeply in love with Laura. I tried hard to keep my feelings hidden, but I suspected that Marian had guessed. I often saw her watching me with an expression almost of pity on her face, which I couldn't understand.

One morning after breakfast, about three months after my arrival at Limmeridge House, Marian asked if she could speak to me privately outside.

We were walking across the garden when the gardener passed us with a letter in his hand. Marian stopped him.

'Is that letter for me?' she asked.

'No, it's for Miss Laura,' answered the man, holding out the letter as he spoke. Marian took it from him and looked at the address.

'That's strange,' she said. 'I don't recognize the handwriting. Who gave this to you?'

'A young woman,' replied the gardener.

'All right,' said Marian. 'Take it to the house and give it to Miss Laura.'

She then led me to the summer house – the same summer house where I had first seen Laura. We went inside and sat down at the small table. I waited, wondering what she would say.

'Mr Hartright,' began Marian, 'I hope you think of me as your friend because I'm going to speak to you now as a friend. I've discovered your secret. I know that you're in love with Laura. I don't blame you and you've done nothing wrong. However there's something I must tell you – something which will cause you great pain. You must leave Limmeridge House at once.'

I felt terribly saddened by her words.

'I know I'm only a poor art teacher,' I began.

'No,' said Marian, 'it's not because you're an art teacher. The reason you must leave is that Laura is going to get married soon, and her future husband is coming here on Monday with his lawyer. Our family lawyer, Mr Gilmore, is coming here too. The two lawyers are going to draw up the marriage settlement between Laura and her husband. Once they have arranged this, a date for the wedding can be fixed.'

Her words felt like arrows shot into my heart. I could hardly move or speak.

'May I know her future husband's name?' I asked at last.

'Sir Percival Glyde,' replied Marian. 'He's from a very good family and has a large house with a lot of land in Hampshire in the south of England. He's a baronet by title.'

Baronet! Suddenly I was reminded of the Woman in White. She had asked me if I knew any baronets and had told me of one who was cruel and wicked. But then, I told myself, there were hundreds of baronets in England. There was no reason to suppose that she meant Sir Percival Glyde.

'I'm so sorry, Mr Hartright,' Marian said gently, 'but I had to tell you. The marriage was arranged two years ago by Laura's father, before he died.'

'I see,' I said. 'Then there is no place for me here. Let me leave Limmeridge House at once. But what reason shall I give to Mr Fairlie as to why I'm going?'

'Don't leave yet,' said Marian. 'Wait until the post arrives tomorrow. Then tell Mr Fairlie you've received a letter from London and that you have to return there at once on urgent business.'

I had just agreed to this plan when we heard footsteps

approaching the summer house. It was Laura's maid.

'Oh, Miss Marian,' said the girl. 'Please can you come quickly to the house. Miss Laura is very upset by a letter she received this morning.'

'It must be the same letter the gardener brought,' said Marian worriedly. 'Come on, let's go.'

We hurried back to the house. I went to my room while Marian went to find Laura.

About half an hour later someone knocked on my door. To my surprise it was Marian, holding a letter in her hand and looking extremely angry and upset.

'Laura has received this,' she said. 'I'd like you to read it. We don't know who it's from – nobody has signed it.'

I took the letter from Marian and read the following.

Do you believe in dreams, Miss Fairlie? I hope you do, because last night I dreamed about you.

You were standing in a church, waiting to be married. You looked beautiful in your lovely white silk wedding dress. Beside you stood the man who was going to be your husband.

He was handsome, about forty-five years old, with dark eyes and a beard. He had a slight cough, and when he put his hand up to his mouth, I could see a thin red mark on the back of his hand.

I could see deep into this man's heart. It was as black as night. On his heart these words were written in letters of blood – This man has done harm to many people, and he will do harm also to this woman.

Behind him was a devil, laughing. And behind you stood an angel, crying.

Listen to my warning, Miss Fairlie. Don't marry this man. Your mother was my first, my best, my only friend. I loved her very much and I love you because of her.

Don't marry this man, Miss Fairlie.

The letter finished as suddenly as it had begun and there was no signature at the end.

'Who is the man?' I asked.

'The description is of Sir Percival Glyde,' replied Marian. 'He's forty-five with a cough and a mark on his hand.'

I read the line again – *Your mother was my first, my best, my only friend*.

'Only one person could have written this,' I said. 'The Woman in White.'

Chapter 4 In the Churchyard

Marian and I looked at each other in astonishment.

'We must find out more about the woman who gave this letter to the gardener,' said Marian. 'Come on.'

We found the gardener at work as usual but he couldn't give us any more information to help us. The woman who had given him the letter had been wearing a long dark-blue coat and a scarf which covered her hair. She hadn't spoken a word to him. After giving him the letter, she had hurried away in the direction of the village.

We then went to the village and spent several hours asking people there if they had seen a strange woman that day, but nobody had. Finally in the afternoon we visited the village school – the same school which Mrs Fairlie, Marian and Laura's mother had set up.

School had just finished for the day and the children had all gone home except for one small boy standing alone in the playground. We asked him if he had seen any strangers in the village that morning, but he shook his head.

'No,' he said, 'but I saw a ghost yesterday evening.'

'Don't tell lies,' said Marian angrily. 'There are no such things as ghosts.'

'But I *did* see one,' said the small boy excitedly. 'It was just where a ghost ought to be – in the churchyard. It was the ghost of a woman, dressed all in white. It was standing by the grave with the tall white cross.'

Marian turned pale and looked me eagerly in the face.

'The Woman in White!' she said. 'And the grave with the tall white cross is my mother's grave. What does she want with that? Let's go at once to the churchyard. Perhaps we can learn something more there.'

We were quite close to the churchyard. The church was a small building of grey stone, and was situated in a peaceful valley. The graves lay behind the church and rose a little way up the hillside. There was a low stone wall all around the graves, and a small stream flowing down from the hillside ran along beside the wall. In one corner of the churchyard there was a group of trees, and near them was a tall white marble cross. Marian pointed to it.

'That cross marks my mother's grave,' she said. 'You go on. I'll go back to the house now. I don't want to leave Laura alone for too long. Let's meet later at the house.'

I approached Mrs Fairlie's grave and examined the white marble cross. Then I noticed something strange. One half of the cross and the stone beneath had been marked and made dirty by bad weather. But the other half was bright and clear as if somebody had cleaned the marble very recently.

'Perhaps whoever has started cleaning the marble will return to finish the job,' I thought. 'I'll wait and see.'

The sun was beginning to go down and a cold wind started to blow from the sea. Dark storm clouds were moving quickly across the sky. In the far distance I could hear the noise of the sea. What a wild and lonely place this was.

I found a hiding place among the trees and began to wait, my eyes on the white marble cross. I waited for about half an hour. The sun had just set when suddenly I saw a figure enter the churchyard and approach the grave hurriedly.

The figure was that of a woman. She was wearing a long coat of a dark-blue colour, but I could see a bit of the dress she wore underneath her coat. My heart began to beat fast as I noticed the colour – white.

The woman approached the grave and stood looking at it for a long time. Then she kissed the cross and took out a cloth from under her coat. She wet the cloth in the stream and started to clean the marble.

She was so busy with what she was doing that she didn't hear me approach her. When I was within a few feet of her, I stopped. She could sense that someone was behind her and stopped cleaning the marble, turning round slowly. When she saw me, she gave a faint cry of terror.

'Don't be frightened,' I said. 'Don't you remember me? We met in London very late one night and I helped you find your way. I acted as your friend then, and I want to be your friend now. Please don't be afraid.'

She continued to look at me with a face full of fear. There was no doubt that it was the same strange woman – the woman I had met on Hampstead Heath.

'What are you doing here?' she whispered at last.

'Do you remember me telling you that I was going to Cumberland? Well, since we last met, I've been living and working at Limmeridge House.'

The woman's sad pale face brightened for a moment.

'Ah, how happy you must be there,' she said.

She smiled and I saw again the extraordinary likeness between her and Laura Fairlie. The great difference was that Laura's face was full of joy and happiness, while this woman's face was sad and frightened. What could it mean?

She was watching me.

'You're looking at me, and you're thinking of something,' she said. 'What is it?'

'Nothing,' I replied. 'Tell me, what's your name? And what are you doing here?'

'My name is Anne Catherick,' she replied. 'And I've come here to be close to my dear friend's grave. Nobody looks after it – see how dirty it is. I must clean it.'

She picked up her cloth and started cleaning the marble.

'Are you staying in the village?' I asked her.

'No,' she replied, 'at a farm about three miles away called Todd's Corner. The people there are good and kind, and look after me well.'

'And where have you come from?' I went on.

'I escaped,' she said. 'I've run away and I'm not going back.'

'Escaped!' I said in astonishment. 'From where?'

'From an asylum – a place where mad people are kept.'

'An asylum! What asylum?' I asked. 'What's its name?'

When she told me its name, I knew it to be in north London, quite near the place where I had met her.

'You don't think I should go back there, do you?' she said, looking at me worriedly. 'I'm not mad and I've done nothing wrong. I was shut up in the asylum by a man who is very cruel and wicked.'

'No, I don't think you should go back there,' I said. 'I'm very glad that you escaped. But what about your family?'

'I have a mother, but she and I don't get on very well. I don't know about my father; I never met him. He's dead, I suppose.'

Suddenly she looked at me with a new expression. 'How's Miss Fairlie?' she asked.

'I'm afraid Miss Fairlie isn't very well or happy,' I said. 'She received your letter this morning. You did write that letter, didn't you, Anne?'

The woman looked very frightened. The small amount of colour she had in her cheeks left her face and she dropped the cloth which she was holding.

15

'You frightened Miss Fairlie badly,' I went on. 'You shouldn't have written that letter. It was very wrong of you. If you had something to say to Miss Fairlie, you should have gone to Limmeridge House and told her yourself.'

Anne sank down on her knees with her arms round the cross.

'I'm very sorry,' she whispered. 'Please ask Miss Fairlie to forgive me. I didn't mean to frighten her, but I had to warn her about the man she's going to marry.'

'Do you mean Sir Percival Glyde?' I asked. 'What harm has he done you?'

At the mention of Sir Percival's name, a look of terrible hatred and fear came over the woman's face. She screamed out, and my heart leaped in terror.

'Sir Percival Glyde is the wicked man who shut me up in the asylum,' she cried.

Then she got to her feet and ran out of the churchyard before I could stop her.

Chapter 5 Anne Catherick Disappears

Half an hour later, I was back at the house and informing Marian about everything that had happened during my meeting with Anne Catherick. Marian listened with great attention.

'I'm so worried about the future,' she said. 'I don't have a very good feeling about Laura's marriage to Sir Percival. What shall we do now?'

'I have a suggestion,' I said. 'We have to ask Anne Catherick a lot more questions, but I'm sure she will talk more openly to a woman than a man. Tomorrow, why don't you come with me to Todd's Corner, the farm where she's staying? You can meet her there and talk to her.'

'Very well,' agreed Marian. 'And in the meantime, there's

something else we have to do. We need to find out *why* Sir Percival Glyde shut Anne Catherick up in the asylum. The asylum you have mentioned is a well-known private one and it's very expensive. Why is Sir Percival Glyde paying all that money to keep Anne there? We need to know the answer to that question before Sir Percival can marry my sister. Laura's happiness means everything to me.

'I'll write to our family lawyer, Mr Gilmore, and tell him what's happened. He's an old friend whom I trust completely and who will advise me as to what to do.'

After breakfast the next morning, when the post had come, I sent a polite note to Mr Fairlie. I told him I had to return to London on urgent business and asked his permission to leave. I knew that my time at Limmeridge House was nearly at an end.

An hour later I received Mr Fairlie's reply.

Dear Mr Hartright,
I'm sorry but I'm not feeling well enough to see you at the moment. Please excuse me. My nerves are so very delicate.

I cannot possibly imagine what business you have in London which is more important than your business at Limmeridge House. I am really very disappointed in you.

However as I do not wish to be upset by any more such requests from you, I will allow you to leave. My health is of the greatest importance. Therefore you may go.
Yours sincerely

Frederick Fairlie

I folded up the note and put it away. I didn't feel any anger towards Mr Fairlie, I was only glad to leave. Then I went downstairs to find Marian and tell her that I was ready to walk to the farmhouse with her to meet Anne Catherick.

We had agreed to say nothing to Laura about my meeting with Anne in the churchyard, and what Anne had said about Sir

Percival Glyde. It would only worry Laura and upset her.

On our way to Todd's Corner we arranged that Marian would enter alone, and I would wait outside. I thought she would be a long time talking to Anne Catherick, but she went into the farmhouse and came put again in less than five minutes.

'Doesn't Anne Catherick want to see you?' I asked in astonishment.

'Anne Catherick has gone,' replied Marian.

'Gone?'

'Yes. The farmer's wife just told me she left for the station at eight o'clock this morning.'

'Let's ask the farmer's wife some more questions,' I said.

We went back inside. Clearly the farmer's wife had no idea why Anne Catherick had left so suddenly. She had been planning to stay at the farm for several more days, but the evening before she had suddenly become ill and fainted.

'Do you think anything happened to frighten her?' I asked.

'I don't think so,' replied the farmer's wife. 'I was only trying to cheer her up by telling her the local news. She looked so pale and sad sometimes that I felt sorry for her. I was telling her about Miss Fairlie and Limmeridge House as I thought she would be interested.'

'Did you tell her that visitors were expected at the house on Monday?' I said.

'Yes, sir. I told her that Sir Percival Glyde was coming. She was taken ill after that. I didn't say anything wrong, did I? I didn't mean to upset her.'

'Don't worry, you did nothing wrong,' Marian said kindly.

As soon as we got outside, we stopped and looked at each other. The expression on Marian's face was very serious.

'Sir Percival Glyde must give us a very good explanation about what has happened between Anne Catherick and himself,' she said, 'or Laura will never be his wife.'

Chapter 6 Mr Gilmore Takes Charge

Just as we were walking round to the front of Limmeridge House, a horse and carriage approached us along the drive and drew up outside the front steps. An old gentleman started to get out of the carriage.

'It's Mr Gilmore, our family lawyer,' said Marian and hurried forward to greet him. She shook hands with him and introduced me before leading him into the house.

Mr Gilmore had a red face and white hair which he wore rather long. He was very neatly dressed in a black coat, waistcoat and trousers. He had an air of kindness and old-fashioned politeness which was very pleasing.

I knew that Marian and Mr Gilmore would have a lot to talk about so I didn't follow them inside. Instead I turned back into the garden and began to wander about alone, along the paths where we had spent so many happy times in the summer.

Now it was winter and everything had changed. The flowers and leaves had all gone, and the earth was bare and cold. Every place I went reminded me of the happy times when I had walked or sat talking with Laura. I remembered her warm smile and her lovely voice and the conversations we had had as we got to know one another. But now there was no Laura and only a frozen emptiness remained.

After a time I could bear it no longer. The empty silence struck my heart cold and I decided to return to the house. I was walking along a path when I saw Mr Gilmore hurrying towards me.

'Just the very person I've been looking for,' he said. 'My dear Mr Hartright, I want to speak to you for a few minutes. Marian and I have been talking over family matters, and of course she has told me about the unpleasant business of the letter which Laura received.

'You have acted well, Mr Hartright, and done everything you

could. You have been of great help to Marian and Laura, and I owe you many thanks for that. Now I want to tell you that I'll take over the matter. It is in safe hands – *my* hands.'

'May I ask what you are going to do?' I said.

'I'm going to send a copy of the letter to Sir Percival Glyde at once. He'll be able to look at it before he comes here. He has an excellent reputation and a very high position in society. I'm sure he'll give us a very satisfactory explanation when he arrives on Monday.'

I wasn't sure if Mr Gilmore was right, but I kept my feelings to myself. There was nothing else I could do.

Mr Gilmore then changed the conversation to general subjects and we walked back to the house together. It was nearly time for dinner so I went to my room and waited there until I heard the dinner bell ring. Then I went downstairs.

I hadn't seen or spoken to Laura all day. And now our last evening together had come.

She was wearing a pretty dark-blue dress – the one which was my favourite. She looked more beautiful than ever – beautiful but sad. She came forward to meet me and gave me her hand with her usual friendliness. She was trying hard to be as normal as possible, but her smile, usually so warm, was very faint and her fingers were as cold as ice.

As we sat through dinner I pretended to be happy, but I felt as if my heart was breaking. Mr Gilmore and Marian did most of the talking. Mr Gilmore noticed nothing wrong and told stories and jokes. Laura sat silently. Now and again her eyes would meet mine, and then she would look away.

At last the meal ended and we all went through to the sitting room. Mr Gilmore and Marian got out the card table and started to play cards. I stood still, not knowing where to go or what to do next, while Laura went to the piano.

'Won't you please sit in your usual place?' she asked me in a low voice. 'Let me play some of the music you like best.'

'Thank you,' I said. 'I'd love to hear you play my favourite music on my last night.'

Laura's face grew pale.

'I'm so very sorry you are going,' she whispered. Her face grew even paler, and she turned away from me quickly.

'I'll remember your kind words long after tomorrow has come and gone,' I said. 'I'll never forget them.'

'Don't speak of tomorrow,' she replied with a sigh. 'Let the music speak to us tonight, in a happier language than ours.'

She sat down and began to play, but she couldn't concentrate; she kept making mistakes and playing the wrong notes. I saw Mr Gilmore look up several times in surprise.

At last the time had come to say goodnight. Mr Gilmore stood up and shook my hand warmly.

'It was a great pleasure to meet you, Mr Hartright,' he said. 'I do hope we'll meet again. And don't worry about that little matter of business which we spoke about. It's quite safe in my hands. Goodbye and have a good journey!'

The next morning I went downstairs at half past seven. Both Marian and Laura were already in the breakfast room, waiting for me. In the cold early morning air and the gloomy light the three of us sat down together and tried to eat and talk. But it was too difficult – our hearts were too sad.

Suddenly Laura got up and ran from the room.

'It's better this way,' said Marian. 'It's better for you and for her.'

I was very disappointed that Laura could let me go without saying goodbye properly.

Marian took my hands and pressed them in her own.

'I'll write to you,' she said. 'You've been like a brother to me and Laura, Walter. Thank you so much for everything. And now you'd better go. I'll watch you leave from upstairs. Goodbye.'

She too left the room and I remained alone for a few minutes, looking sadly out of the window at the winter scene outside.

Then I heard the door open again and the soft sound of a woman's dress moving over the carpet. My heart beat quickly as I turned round. It was Laura, holding something in her hand.

'I only went to get this,' she said, holding out a little sketch. 'I hope it will remind you of your friends here.'

It was drawn in her own hand and was of the summer house where we'd first met. My hand trembled as I took it from her. I was afraid to say what I really felt, so I just said, 'It will never leave me – it will stay beside me for the rest of my life.'

'Please promise me something. Promise me that if ever a time comes when you need help, you will remember me – the poor drawing master who taught you. Promise you'll let me know.'

'I promise,' she replied. 'I promise with all my heart. Oh, please don't look at me like that.'

I had moved closer to her and taken her hand in mine. I held her hand fast and looked into her eyes while the tears were flowing down her cheeks.

'For God's sake, leave me!' she cried out.

At that moment I knew that Laura loved me too.

I dropped her hand. Through the tears which blinded my own eyes, I saw her for the last time. She sank into a chair with her arms on the table and her head resting on them.

One last look and I left the room. The door closed behind me for ever. Already Laura Fairlie was a memory of the past.

The story is continued by Mr Vincent Gilmore, lawyer

Chapter 7 Sir Percival Explains

I arrived at Limmeridge House one afternoon in November. The purpose of my visit was to meet with Miss Laura Fairlie's future husband, Sir Percival Glyde, after which I would return to

London and draw up the marriage settlement.

I've been lawyer to the Fairlie family for many years. I knew Laura's father, Mr Philip Fairlie, very well, and I've known Marian and Laura since they were children. I'm very fond of them both, and I was most anxious to make a good marriage settlement for Laura.

On arriving at Limmeridge House, I was introduced to Mr Walter Hartright, the art teacher, who seemed a very pleasant young man. I was informed that Mr Hartright was leaving the next day. Marian also told me about the business of the letter which Laura had received, and how helpful Mr Hartright had been to her about that. I told them that I would send a copy of the letter to Sir Percival.

Laura, I'm sorry to say, didn't look well – not like her usual happy self at all. She played the piano to us that evening, but she made a lot of mistakes.

The following day Mr Hartright left very early in the morning. The rest of the weekend passed quietly and on Monday Sir Percival Glyde arrived.

I have seldom met such a charming and friendly man. When we were introduced, I found his manner so easy and pleasant that straight away we got on together like old friends.

However I was surprised to see that Laura didn't seem very happy to see him. After his arrival, she left the room as soon as she could politely do so, leaving Marian and I to speak with Sir Percival.

As soon as the door had closed behind Laura, Sir Percival brought up the business of the letter. He had received the copy which I had sent him and, as I had expected, he had a very satisfactory explanation.

He told us that several years ago he had had a servant called Mrs Catherick who was excellent in every way and had provided him with loyal and faithful service through difficult times.

Mrs Catherick's husband had left her, and she had one little daughter called Anne. Unfortunately ever since she was a small child, Anne had had mental problems – there was something wrong with her mind – so that she didn't behave like a normal person. These problems got so bad that in the end her mother could no longer look after her at home.

Sir Percival offered to help by finding and placing Anne in an excellent asylum where people would be kind to her and where she would be well looked after. It was expensive to keep Anne in the asylum, but because of Mrs Catherick's loyal service to him, he offered to pay the money.

Unfortunately Anne had found out that Sir Percival had had something to do with placing her in the asylum. She hadn't understood that he was acting out of kindness to help her mother and herself. She hated him because he had placed her there so she had written the letter to Laura.

When Sir Percival had finished, I said, 'Now everything is very clear and I understand completely. Thank you, Sir Percival. How kind of you it was to help Mrs Catherick's poor daughter.'

To my surprise Marian seemed to show some hesitation. Sir Percival was also quick to notice this.

'My dear Marian,' he said. 'I know you still have some doubts about this matter, so let me make a suggestion. Please write to Mrs Catherick yourself and ask her two questions – if she knew that Anne was placed in the asylum, and if she was pleased about the help which I gave her.'

Marian looked a little embarrassed, but she agreed. She went over to the writing table, where she wrote the note quickly. Sir Percival gave her Mrs Catherick's address, then Marian called a servant and gave the note to him to post.

'Good,' said Sir Percival. 'Now, if you have no objections, I'd like to ask some questions myself. I'm most anxious to find Anne Catherick. We must help the poor woman by returning her to

Marian looked a little embarrassed, but she agreed. She went over to the writing table, where she wrote the note quickly.

the asylum as soon as possible. Marian, did you or Laura actually speak to her yourselves?'

'No,' replied Marian, 'she spoke only to Mr Hartright.'

'Mr Hartright? Who's Mr Hartright?'

'He was our art teacher. He's left us now and gone back to London.'

'I must get in touch with Mr Hartright,' said Sir Percival. 'Do you have his address? He may have some useful information about Anne. Where did you say she was staying when she was here?'

'At a farmhouse called Todd's Corner,' said Marian.

'I'll go there at once,' said Sir Percival. 'Perhaps she said something to the people there which will help us find her.' Then he left the room in a great hurry.

'Don't you believe Sir Percival's explanation?' I asked Marian. She shook her head slowly.

'I don't know,' she said. 'It makes sense . . . and yet something isn't quite right. But I don't know what.'

Two days later, a short note from Mrs Catherick arrived.

Dear Madam,

Thank you for your letter. It is quite true that my daughter, Anne, was placed in an asylum by Sir Percival Glyde and that I was quite happy with this arrangement. I was grateful to Sir Percival for his help.

Yours sincerely

Jane Catherick

'Now, Marian,' I said, 'you must agree there can be no further doubt about Sir Percival.'

'I suppose not,' said Marian, but she still didn't look very happy. 'Now I must go and tell Laura everything.'

Later that day I saw Laura myself. She looked so pale and sad that I was quite worried about her.

'Please tell me, my dear,' I said as gently as I could. 'Is there something wrong? Aren't you happy about your marriage to Sir Percival? If you aren't, we can try to stop it.'

'Oh, no,' said Laura. 'I promised my father on his deathbed that I would marry Sir Percival and I won't break my promise. You must excuse me – I haven't been very well lately; that's why I'm so weak and nervous.'

I felt sorry for Laura with all my heart but that same afternoon I had to go back to London. Sir Percival very kindly saw me to my carriage.

'I do hope you'll visit me at my house,' he said. 'Such an old friend of the Fairlie family will be welcome any time.'

A charming man indeed – a real gentleman! I couldn't find a fault with him. So why, as my carriage drove away to the station, did I share Marian's feeling that something wasn't right? Why, in my heart, didn't I want to draw up the marriage settlement between Sir Percival and Laura?

Chapter 8 The Marriage Settlement

A week after I returned to London, I received a short letter from Marian, saying that Laura would definitely accept Sir Percival Glyde as her husband. The wedding was due to take place towards the end of December. Marian also said that she was taking Laura away for a short holiday to visit friends in Yorkshire.

On receiving Marian's letter, I started to prepare the marriage settlement for Laura.

The following March Laura would be twenty-one years old. On her twenty-first birthday she would receive a very large sum of money – twenty thousand pounds – which her father had left to her when he died two years ago. This money had been kept for her until she came of age – in other words, until she was twenty-one.

The most important part of Laura's marriage settlement

concerned what would happen to this twenty thousand pounds if Laura died before her husband.

If she had children, clearly the money would all go to the children. But if she had no children, the situation was more complicated.

While I was at Limmeridge House, I had asked Laura what she wished to do with her twenty thousand pounds if she died before Sir Percival. Laura had immediately replied that she wanted the money to go to her half-sister, Marian.

It seemed right and fair to me that Laura's money should return to her family. I therefore drew up the marriage settlement according to her wishes and sent a copy of the document to Sir Percival Glyde's lawyer.

Two days later the document was returned to me. The lawyer had written the following words on it in red ink.

I regret to inform you that Sir Percival Glyde cannot accept what you are proposing. He insists that if his wife, Lady Glyde, dies without leaving children, the whole of her twenty thousand pounds must go to himself.

I was extremely worried by this. It meant that if Laura died before Sir Percival, all her money would go into the pockets of her husband. I wrote a note back immediately, saying that I could not possibly accept such a thing.

Later that day, Sir Percival's lawyer, Mr Merriman, visited me – a fat smiling man who pretended to be very friendly.

'I'm sorry, Mr Gilmore,' he said, 'but Sir Percival is absolutely insisting that the money go to him.'

I thought quickly. The only thing I could do was to play for time, so I said, 'Today's Friday. I'll give you an answer on Tuesday.'

I was very fond of Laura and I knew I had to help her. Her father had been a dear friend who was very good to me. I had to do my best for his only child – I couldn't let all her money go to her husband if that wasn't what she wanted.

Laura was still under age – she wasn't yet twenty-one – so she was still under the protection of her uncle, Mr Frederick Fairlie.

If Mr Fairlie objected to the marriage settlement, it couldn't go ahead. I therefore decided to travel to Limmeridge House and talk to Mr Fairlie. I was sure I could make him see that this marriage settlement wasn't in Laura's best interests.

The next day I left London by an early train and arrived at Limmeridge House in time for dinner. Marian and Laura were away in Yorkshire, and the house was very empty and dull.

I sent a message to Mr Fairlie to say that I had arrived. I received a note back from him to say that my unexpected visit had been a great shock and unfortunately he didn't feel well enough to see me that evening. But he would be pleased to see me at ten o'clock the next morning.

I slept very badly that night. A strong wind blew loudly around the house, and the noise kept me awake. So I wasn't in a very good mood when I went to see Mr Fairlie the next morning. When I went into his sitting room, he was sitting in his usual chair.

I explained to him as clearly as I could how worried I was about Laura's marriage settlement. I told him that Sir Percival was insisting Laura's money all go to him after Laura's death.

'Sir Percival has no legal claim to Laura's money,' I said. 'Laura wants her money to go to Marian after her death. You can help us, Mr Fairlie. If you decide to object to the marriage settlement, Sir Percival must give in or people will say that he's only marrying Laura for her money.'

When I had finished, Mr Fairlie shut his eyes and sighed.

'Dear Gilmore,' he said, 'I don't understand why you've come here to upset me. My nerves are very delicate, you know. Please don't upset me any more.

'Laura isn't yet twenty-one. How is it possible that she should die before Sir Percival Glyde, who is forty-five?

'Gilmore, two things are very important to me – peace and

quiet. I don't want you coming here to disturb me. Please leave the marriage settlement as it is.'

I felt very disappointed and angry with Mr Fairlie. I couldn't believe his selfishness.

'Mr Fairlie,' I said. 'Don't you care about your niece? Don't you care about what is good for her?'

'Please, Gilmore,' said Mr Fairlie, 'don't be so heartless. Can't you see you are upsetting me? I tell you again, leave the marriage settlement as it is. Agree to everything that Sir Percival wants, then we'll have peace and quiet. Now if you'll excuse me, I'm very tired. The servants will give you lunch downstairs before you go back to London.'

I walked to the door. Before I left the room, I turned round and said, 'Whatever happens in the future, Mr Fairlie, remember that I warned you. Remember my words.'

I didn't stay for lunch, but returned to London on the afternoon train. The following Tuesday I told Sir Percival's lawyer that we would accept his wishes. I had no choice.

But in my heart I felt great sorrow and anxiety about the future. No daughter of mine would have been married to any man in the world under the marriage settlement which I was forced to make for Laura Fairlie.

The story is continued by Marian Halcombe

Chapter 9 Laura Prepares for the Wedding

When Mr Gilmore had returned to London after his meeting with Sir Percival Glyde at Limmeridge House, I became more and more anxious about Laura.

I knew that Laura was in love with Walter Hartright. I knew that she didn't want to marry Sir Percival but I also knew very well that she wouldn't break her promise to her dead father. That was why she was insisting on going ahead with the wedding, even if it made her unhappy.

Walter Hartright had given her a little book containing some of his drawings and every night she slept with this book under her pillow. I couldn't bear to see how sad she had become.

'Laura,' I said with great sorrow in my heart. 'You must forget Walter Hartright now. You're going to marry Sir Percival. You must try and think of your new life with him.'

'You're right, dear Marian,' she replied. 'I must say goodbye to this little book for ever.' She then cut off a piece of her lovely golden hair, placed it in the book and gave it to me. 'If Walter ever asks you about me, tell him I'm well and never say I'm unhappy. If I die, promise you'll give him this little book with my hair in it. And say, Marian – oh, say for me what I can never say for myself – that I loved him.' She threw her arms round my neck and began to cry.

The next day a letter arrived for me from Walter, begging me to help him. He said he wanted to find some work far away from England which would take him to new scenes and new people, so that he could try and forget the past and Laura.

I was anxious about Laura and I was also anxious about Walter. Immediately I wrote to two old friends of my mother's – both men who held high positions in society and who would be able to find Walter some work.

Meanwhile, Sir Percival had left us to return to his own house. I wrote a short letter to Mr Gilmore in London, informing him that the marriage was definitely going ahead.

A few days later, I received another letter from Walter. He thanked me for helping him, and said that one of my mother's friends had offered him a place on an expedition to Central America. His ship was due to sail on 21 December and he expected to be away from England for about eighteen months.

I decided not to say anything to Laura about this. From what Walter said in his letter, the expedition was going to be dangerous. If I told her, it would only upset her more.

I suggested to Laura that we visit some old friends in Yorkshire as I thought the change of air would do her good. She agreed and we spent a happy week there. However we were then called back to Limmeridge by a letter from Mr Fairlie, commanding us to return at once.

As soon as I got back to Limmeridge, I went to Mr Fairlie's room. He informed me that he had had a letter from Sir Percival Glyde, proposing the date of 22 December for the wedding. This was in only four weeks' time.

'Please, dear Marian, tell Laura to get ready for the wedding,' said Mr Fairlie. 'I'm afraid I can't because, as you know, my nerves are very delicate. You're very lucky that your nerves are so strong. Thank you so much, Marian, and please don't bang the door on your way out!'

I went immediately to find Laura. When I told her the news, her face turned very pale and she began to tremble. She cried out, 'Not so soon, Marian, oh, not so soon!'

'Very well,' I said. 'I'm going to tell your uncle and Sir Percival that they can't have everything their own way.'

I was just going out of the door when Laura stopped me.

'No, Marian,' she said. 'What's the use? I've caused enough trouble and anxiety to everyone. I don't want to cause any more. Tell my uncle I agree to the date. It makes no difference to me.'

My heart felt as if it would break when I heard her words. I went back to Mr Fairlie, feeling angry and upset. When I got to the door of his room, I opened it and shouted inside, 'Tell Sir Percival that Laura agrees to the twenty-second!'

After that I banged the door as loudly as possible and went downstairs, feeling a little better. I really hoped that Mr Fairlie's nerves would be damaged for the rest of the day.

Now the preparations for the wedding began. The dressmaker came to measure Laura for her wedding dress but although Laura tried hard to be interested, I could see that she wasn't. How different and how excited she would be, I thought sadly, if she was going to marry Walter.

After the wedding, Sir Percival planned to take Laura to Italy for six months. He had arranged to meet up with an old friend of his there, Count Fosco. In June they were all going to come back to Sir Percival's home, Blackwater House. I would live there with them too, and I was certainly very grateful that I could still be close to Laura.

On 20 December, two days before the wedding, Sir Percival arrived at Limmeridge House, bringing with him some really beautiful jewellery for Laura. He appeared to be very happy and didn't seem to notice how pale and quiet Laura was.

The next morning, while I was out walking, I took the road that led to the farmhouse at Todd's Corner where Anne Catherick had stayed. To my surprise I saw Sir Percival coming towards me from the farmhouse. When we met, he told me he had been to the farm to ask if there had been any news of Anne, but the farmer's wife had told him there was none.

'I'm most anxious to find the poor woman,' he said. 'She should be in the care of the asylum again, where she'll be safe. Do you happen to know if the art teacher, Mr Hartright, has seen her again?'

'He hasn't seen her since he left here,' I replied.

'How very sad,' said Sir Percival in a disappointed voice. Yet he didn't look disappointed at all. He looked relieved.

Why was Sir Percival so keen to find Anne Catherick on the day before his wedding, I wondered? Then I put the thought out of my head. It must be because he was really worried about her safety and wanted to help her.

The twenty-second of December came. The weather that day was terrible – wild and stormy. Laura and Sir Percival were married at eleven o'clock in the morning, and left for Italy at three o'clock in the afternoon.

Up to the last moment, I had been hoping against hope that something would happen to stop the wedding. But nothing did.

PART TWO

Chapter 1 At Blackwater Park

It was six months later, and I had just arrived at Blackwater Park, Sir Percival Glyde's home. Laura and Sir Percival were due to return the following day from Italy. They would be accompanied by Sir Percival's old friend, Count Fosco, who was going to stay at Blackwater Park too.

I was impatient to see Laura's dear face again – the past six months had passed so slowly. I had received several letters from her, but it was quite impossible to tell whether she was any happier. She hardly mentioned Sir Percival or whether he treated her kindly. Instead she wrote about the wonderful cities she had visited – Florence, Rome and Venice.

I had also received one short letter from Walter Hartright, saying that the expedition had landed safely in Central America. There had been no more news or information about Anne Catherick – it seemed she had completely disappeared.

So now here I was waiting at Blackwater Park. In the morning the housekeeper, a kind and friendly lady called Mrs Michelson, showed me over the house. The main part of the house was very old, and full of dark gloomy corridors with ugly family pictures of Sir Percival's ancestors.

After lunch I decided to explore the grounds outside. The house was surrounded by trees – in my opinion, far too many trees – all young and planted closely together so that they shut

34

the house and garden in. It was so different from the wide open spaces of Limmeridge House which I was used to.

There was a path leading down through the trees and I followed it. After some time, the path opened out on to a small sandy beach beside a lake. This was Blackwater Lake, which gave the house its name. The water by the beach was clear and still, but on the other side the trees came right down to the edge of the lake and their shadows made it look black and poisonous. It was a gloomy place.

An old wooden boathouse stood at the side of the beach. On approaching it, I found that there were a few chairs and a small table inside. I entered and sat down for a little while to rest.

I had been in the boathouse for only a few minutes when I heard a sad kind of noise, as of an animal in great pain. It was coming from under the seat and when I looked down, I saw a poor little dog there. On looking closer, I noticed that one of its sides was covered in blood. It had been shot.

Immediately I lifted the poor little dog in my arms as gently as I could. I folded my skirt round it and carried it back to the house where I went to find the housekeeper.

The moment Mrs Michelson saw the dog, she said in surprise, 'Why, that's Mrs Catherick's dog!'

I nearly dropped the dog in my astonishment. 'What!' I said. 'Has Mrs Catherick been here?'

'Yes,' replied Mrs Michelson. 'She came here yesterday asking for news of her daughter, Anne. Someone had told her they had seen a young woman of Anne's description in this neighbourhood, but she couldn't find out any more. I suppose the dog must have wandered off and got lost. Where was it?'

'In the old boathouse that looks out over the lake.'

'I expect Sir Percival's gamekeeper, Baxter, shot it,' said Mrs Michelson. 'When he finds strange dogs wandering about, he always shoots them. Poor little thing!'

At that moment the dog gave one last faint cry and died in my arms. Its suffering was finally over.

I was still feeling astonished about Mrs Catherick's visit. I wanted to gain as much information as I could about her.

'Do you know where Mrs Catherick lives?' I asked.

'Yes,' replied Mrs Michelson. 'In a village called Welmingham, about twenty miles from here.'

'I suppose you know her well?'

'No, not at all. Yesterday was the first time I saw her. I'd heard of her, of course, because I'd heard of Sir Percival's kindness in putting her daughter under medical care. But she asked me not to tell Sir Percival she'd been here. Don't you think that was rather strange?'

I did indeed. Sir Percival had certainly given me the impression, in our conversation at Limmeridge House, that he and Mrs Catherick knew each other well. Why would she not want him to know of her visit? It didn't make sense.

I had kept the short note from Mrs Catherick which she had written in answer to my letter enquiring about Anne. One of these days, I thought, I would go over to Welmingham with the note. I would introduce myself to Mrs Catherick and have a chat with her. I had questions which needed answers, and one of them was why she wanted her visit to Blackwater Park kept secret from Sir Percival Glyde.

Moreover, was it possible that Anne *was* still in the neighbourhood after all?

Chapter 2 Mr Merriman Brings News

The following day, Sir Percival and Laura, accompanied by Count Fosco, returned to Blackwater Park.

To my sorrow, I found great changes in Laura, or Lady Glyde as she now was. She was still beautiful, and still as loving and kind as ever, but her face had lost its happy innocent look, and there was a secret sadness in her eyes. Whenever I tried to ask her questions about her married life, she would stop me by putting her finger gently on my lips, and changing the subject.

'Dear Marian,' she said, 'I don't want to make you unhappy by telling you about things which will upset you. We're together again – let's just be grateful for that.'

She asked me if I had heard any news of Walter Hartright, but I told her I hadn't. I could see from the expression on her face that she was still in love with him.

As for Sir Percival Glyde, I found that he too had changed over the past few months. When he had visited us at Limmeridge House, before he married Laura, he had been very charming to all of us – to Laura, to myself, to Mr Fairlie and to Mr Gilmore. But now that he had got what he wanted and married Laura, there was no need for him to be charming any more. His manner to me was no longer polite, but cool and rude. He was often in a bad temper, and little things would annoy him.

And what about Sir Percival's friend, Count Fosco?

I have to admit that he was a most attractive, interesting and fascinating man. I didn't trust him and I didn't want to like him, but I couldn't help myself.

Count Fosco was Italian by birth, but he had lived in England for a long time and spoke English perfectly.

He was a huge fat man of about sixty years old. He loved fine clothes and had many colourful and expensive shirts and waistcoats. Moreover, he was a most interesting man who could talk in a fascinating way about a great variety of subjects. But not only could he talk, he also knew how to listen, especially to women. He had a gift of making a woman feel that she was the most special person in the world.

Count Fosco loved small animals and birds and had a number of pet white mice which travelled everywhere with him in a special cage. Sometimes he would let them out of the cage and then they would run all over his huge fat body and sit in pairs on his shoulders.

It was obvious too that the Count had a very strong influence over his friend, Sir Percival. Sir Percival wasn't as clever as the Count and clearly he was afraid of him.

I too was afraid of the Count. I knew that whatever happened, I mustn't make an enemy of him. He would be a far more dangerous enemy than Sir Percival. I was afraid of his eyes – they were cold and clear and shone with an extraordinary power. When I looked into them, I felt that he could make me do anything he wanted.

A few days after Sir Percival and Laura's return, we were sitting having lunch when a servant entered the dining room.

'Mr Merriman has just come, Sir Percival,' said the servant, 'and wishes to see you immediately.'

Sir Percival's face changed colour and he looked at the man with an expression of great anger and alarm.

'Mr Merriman!' he repeated.

'Yes, Sir Percival,' said the man. 'Mr Merriman from London. He's in the library.'

Sir Percival left the table and hurried out of the room.

'Who's Mr Merriman?' asked Laura in surprise. 'What does his visit here mean?'

Before I could say anything, Count Fosco quietly replied, 'Mr Merriman is Sir Percival's lawyer. And his visit here means that something has happened. He brings unexpected news for Sir Percival – news that is either very good or very bad, but certainly not ordinary.'

We waited, but Sir Percival didn't return to the dining room. I decided to go for a walk after lunch, and went upstairs to get my hat and coat. Just as I was about to come downstairs again, I heard the library door open below me, and saw Sir Percival and Mr Merriman coming out.

'Everything depends on your wife, Sir Percival,' Mr Merriman was saying seriously. 'If she signs the document, you can get hold of her money now. If not, then there will be serious problems because the debt you owe is almost due.'

I understood everything very clearly. Sir Percival was going to try and obtain Laura's twenty thousand pounds to clear his debts. But to do so he needed Laura's signature to show that she gave her permission for him to use her money. I crept back upstairs to Laura's room at once to tell her what I'd heard. To my surprise, she didn't seem upset.

'That's just what I thought,' she said. 'Sir Percival hasn't got enough money of his own and he can't wait until I'm dead. He wants me to sign my money over to him now.'

'Promise me, Laura, that you won't sign anything without looking at it very carefully first?'

'I promise, Marian. I'll do nothing which I might have cause to regret one day. Don't worry.'

Chapter 3 Sir Percival is Angry

That evening Sir Percival was once again very charming to Laura, treating her in the same kind and loving way as he had at Limmeridge House. But he didn't mention anything about the document she would have to sign.

After breakfast the next morning Laura and I got ready to go out for a walk.

'Where are you going?' asked Sir Percival at once.

'We were thinking of walking to the lake,' replied Laura.

'Then Fosco and I will join you,' said Sir Percival. 'It's such a beautiful morning for a walk.'

This was very surprising and unusual. All the time we had been together at Blackwater Park, Sir Percival and Count Fosco had never wanted to come with us on any walks.

The Count, who was wearing a bright-blue shirt and a colourful hat, said, 'I'll bring my family with me. My dear little white mice don't want to be left alone in the house. There are dogs here and I don't want them to be frightened.'

We all walked down to the lake and sat down to rest in the boathouse. The Count, who had been carrying his mice in their cage, opened the door so that they could come out and run over him as usual. Sir Percival didn't sit down, but stood nervously at the door, looking out across the lake.

Suddenly Count Fosco gave a cry.

'One of my dear little mice has got lost!' he said. 'There should be five of them, and I can see only four.'

'There it is, under the seat,' I said.

'Thank you, my dear Miss Halcombe.' The Count got down on his knees and took the little animal up in his hand. Then he suddenly stopped and looked at the ground in front of him. When he rose to his feet again, his hand was shaking and he said in a whisper, 'Percival! Come here and look at this!'

'What's the matter?' asked Sir Percival, coming inside.

'There's a bloodstain on the floor here,' said the Count.

'Blood!' said Laura, turning to me with a look of terror.

'It's all right,' I said. 'It's only the blood of a poor little dog. I found it dying here on the day before you all returned from abroad. The poor thing had been shot.'

'Whose dog was it?' asked Sir Percival. 'One of mine?'

I hesitated. I remembered that Mrs Catherick hadn't wanted Sir Percival to find out about her visit to Blackwater Park, but I had to give him an answer.

'The housekeeper said it was Mrs Catherick's dog,' I said.

Sir Percival pushed his way into the boathouse and stood in front of me with an expression of astonishment and anger.

'Mrs Catherick has been here?' he said. 'What the devil did

When Count Fosco rose to his feet again, his hand was shaking and he said in a whisper, 'Percival! Come here and look at this!'

Mrs Catherick want at my house?'

I turned away silently. At that moment Count Fosco stepped forward and put his hand on Sir Percival's shoulder.

'My dear Percival,' he said gently. 'Why don't you go and ask the housekeeper these questions, not Miss Halcombe?'

'Of course,' said Sir Percival, taking a deep breath. 'I apologize for my rude behaviour, Miss Halcombe. I just wanted to know why Mrs Catherick came here.'

With these words he left, and the three of us walked back slowly to the house. When we arrived there, we saw Sir Percival's horse and carriage standing outside all ready to go on a journey. Then Sir Percival himself came out.

'You must excuse me,' he said. 'I'm afraid I have to leave you. Something urgent has come up which I have to attend to, but I'll be back tomorrow. But before I go, there's a small business matter to be settled. Laura, will you come into the library? This won't take a minute. I just need you to sign a document. And you, Miss Halcombe, and Fosco, I need you to act as witnesses to Laura's signature.'

We all followed Sir Percival into the library and sat down round the table. He then opened a cupboard and took out a document which he put in front of Laura, although as it was all folded up she couldn't read any of it. Then he handed her a pen and pointed to the place where he wanted her to sign.

Laura's face was pale, but she showed no fear.

'Please explain to me, Sir Percival,' she said, 'what this document is which you wish me to sign.'

'I haven't got time to explain,' replied her husband. 'My horse is waiting outside. Just sign it, will you!'

But Laura did not move. 'I'm sorry,' she said, 'I want to help, but I can't sign anything unless I know what it is.'

Sir Percival stepped forward, looking so angry that I thought for a moment he was going to hit Laura. Once again Count

Fosco saved the situation.

'My dear Percival,' he said, 'Lady Glyde is quite right. She needs to know *why* she is signing the document. May I make a suggestion? You're in a hurry now – you have to go. Let this matter wait until your return tomorrow.'

Sir Percival looked at his watch. He needed Laura's signature, but he was also anxious to start his journey. He thought for a moment and then got up from his chair.

'Very well!' he said, giving his wife a dark look. 'But you had better sign it tomorrow!'

We heard the wheels of the carriage as Sir Percival drove off. He was going at full speed. Why was he in such a hurry?

'Where has he gone to, Marian?' whispered Laura. 'Everything he does these days seems to frighten me.'

'I'm sure he's gone to visit Mrs Catherick,' I said. 'He was very angry that she came here. But I don't know why.'

Chapter 4 The Figure by the Lake

That evening Laura suggested going out for a walk, and once again we found ourselves walking in the direction of the lake. The air was still and heavy, and when we got to the boathouse we were very glad to sit down and rest inside.

A white fog hung low over the lake. The silence all around was horrible – there was no sound of any bird or movement of the trees.

'How gloomy it is,' said Laura. 'But at least we can be alone here – more so than in any other place at Blackwater Park. Oh, Marian, I'm so unhappy.'

Laura then began to tell me about her marriage, and her relationship with Sir Percival Glyde. She told me many things that made my heart very sad and heavy within me, as I realized how cruelly he treated her. One thing was very clear to me – Sir Percival had never loved Laura, but had married her for her money, and her money alone.

I also felt the most terrible sense of guilt. I was the person responsible for separating Laura from Walter Hartright, the man who loved her. I had encouraged him to leave England, to go far away to a dangerous place from which he might never return. I was responsible for wasting two young lives – Laura's and Walter's – and I had done all this so that she should keep her promise to Sir Percival Glyde, a man who didn't love her and who was cruel to her.

I put my arms round Laura and held her tight. I felt her kisses as she tried to comfort me, and at last she said, 'Come, Marian, it's getting late. Let's go back.'

We got up and went towards the boathouse door. Suddenly Laura turned towards me, her eyes wide with alarm.

'Look!' she exclaimed.

A figure was walking along by the side of the lake, but whether of man or woman, it was impossible to tell. It moved silently and disappeared into the fog.

'I'm so frightened,' whispered Laura. 'Who can it be? Do you think it will follow us back to the house?'

'There's no need to be frightened,' I replied. 'It's probably only someone from the village out walking late. Come on, let's go.'

It was difficult to find the path back to the house in the darkness. All the way back, we had a very strange feeling that someone or something was following us. At one time we thought we heard footsteps, but on turning round we couldn't see anything because of the fog. We walked so quickly that we were out of breath by the time we got back to the house.

I went immediately to the library. I was curious to know where Count Fosco had spent the evening, but he was sitting by the fire reading a book. Clearly he couldn't have been the

44

mysterious figure down by the boathouse – he could never have got back to the house in time. The servants and the housekeeper too were all in their rooms.

The next morning Laura told me that she had lost a little bracelet which I had given her for a wedding present. She said she was sure she had dropped it in the boathouse, and was going to look for it there.

I knew that Sir Percival was expected back that afternoon, and that he would immediately try to force Laura to sign the document again. I was extremely worried about this, and went to my room to try to work out what we should do.

The day was hot and I wasn't feeling very well, so I lay down on my bed and soon fell asleep. I had very strange and disturbing dreams, all about Walter Hartright. Suddenly I was woken by a hand on my shoulder. It was Laura, on her knees by my bed. Her face was full of a wild excitement and her eyes were shining. I looked at her, astonished.

'What's happened?' I asked. 'Has something frightened you?'

She looked round at the door, put her lips close to my ear and whispered in an excited voice, 'Marian – the figure at the lake – the footsteps last night. I've just seen her! I've just spoken to her!'

'Who, for heaven's sake?'

'Anne Catherick!'

I was so astonished that I couldn't speak.

'I have such things to tell you,' Laura went on. 'But come away – we may be interrupted here. Let's go to my room where nobody can hear us.' She took my hand, led me to her room and locked the door. Then she held out her hand and I saw the bracelet which she had lost on her wrist again.

'Anne Catherick found it,' she said. 'I was in the boathouse and was down on my knees looking for it, when a voice said, "Miss Fairlie!" I looked up to see who was calling me by my old unmarried name. There, looking at me from the doorway, was a woman I'd never seen before – a young woman, dressed all in white. She was holding out her hand to me, and in it lay my lost bracelet.

'"Please let me put this on your wrist," she said. "Your dear mother would have let me. I knew her well, when you and I were children. I knew you too, but you don't remember me."

'As I looked at her, I had the strangest feeling. It came to me suddenly that she and I were very like each other. Her face was much thinner and paler than mine, but she looked just as I would look after a long illness.

'"Why did you call me Miss Fairlie?" I asked her. "I'm Lady Glyde now."

'"Because I love the name of Fairlie and hate the name of Glyde," she said. "I tried to save you from marrying that devil. I did my best to prevent you from making a terrible mistake. I wrote you that letter but I didn't do enough. I should have talked to you in person, but I was too afraid."

'She then hid her face in her hands and started to cry. It was terrible to see her and hear her.

'"I wanted to speak to you last night," she said. "I followed you back to the house."

'"What do you want to tell me?" I asked her gently.

'"Listen," she said. "I know a secret about your cruel husband, which if ever it is found out will destroy him. It's a terrible secret – dark and deep. My mother knows it too. That's why he shut me up in the asylum for mad people, where nobody would believe me. But I've escaped, and he's afraid of me. I'll tell you his secret, so then he'll be afraid of you too, and he'll have no more power over you."

'"What secret, Anne? Tell me the secret," I said.

'But then a change came over her face and she ran to the boathouse door. I followed her and put my hand on her arm.

'"We're not alone," she said. "Somebody is out there, watching us. I must go. Come here again tomorrow at this time, and I'll tell you. Be sure to come here by yourself."

'With these words, she pushed me back inside the boathouse and ran off into the trees outside.'

Chapter 5 A Meeting is Postponed

When Laura had finished her astonishing story, I said, 'Listen, Laura. It's of the greatest importance that you keep your appointment at the boathouse with Anne Catherick tomorrow. We must find out what this secret is. But this time I'll follow you there. Anne has escaped Walter, and she has escaped you, but she will not escape me.'

'Do you believe there really *is* a secret, Marian?'

'Certainly I do. And I think Sir Percival is frightened. He knows that if anyone finds out, it will destroy him.'

I left Laura and went downstairs. I was extremely anxious to know where Count Fosco had been that afternoon – could he have been anywhere near the boathouse? Could he have been the person listening to Laura and Anne's conversation? Or had Anne just imagined she heard someone?

Count Fosco wasn't in the house, so I went out into the grounds. I was walking down the path which led to the lake when suddenly the Count appeared in front of me, coming from the opposite direction. I was so shocked by his unexpected appearance that at first I couldn't speak.

'You look surprised to see me, Miss Halcombe,' he said. 'It was such a lovely morning that I decided to go for a walk.'

Immediately I became very suspicious. Count Fosco never took any exercise and certainly *never* went for walks.

'Are you going back to the house?' he went on, taking hold of my arm. 'Do let me come with you. It's such a very great pleasure to have your company.'

As we came within sight of the house, we saw Sir Percival's horse and carriage standing outside. He had just returned and came forward to meet us, still in a bad temper.

'There you are!' he said angrily. 'Where the devil *is* everyone? Where is my wife? Tell her to come down at once.'

'Now just a moment, Percival,' said Count Fosco quietly. He dropped my arm, took Sir Percival's and led him inside. 'I want to have five minutes' conversation with you, about a serious matter of business that very much concerns you.'

I went upstairs to tell Laura that her husband had returned, and would soon be insisting once again that she sign the document. We were sitting together when someone knocked softly at the door. It was Count Fosco, smiling.

'Dear ladies, I bring you good news,' he said. 'News that I'm sure will be a great relief to you. I've persuaded Percival to change his mind. There's no need for you to sign the document now.' He then went out, closing the door.

Laura and I looked at each other in astonishment.

'What can this mean?' Laura asked. 'I thought Sir Percival wanted my money.'

'Maybe Count Fosco has another plan,' was all I could say.

The next day it was raining heavily. Laura and I had agreed that she should go to the boathouse after lunch to meet Anne Catherick, and I should follow her a few minutes later. We didn't want to frighten Anne by arriving together.

Sir Percival went out shortly after breakfast. He had his coat and high boots on, but he didn't tell anyone where he was going. He had still not returned by lunchtime.

Laura left the lunch table as we had planned, and I waited for a short while then followed her. I walked quickly through the trees. When I reached the boathouse, I stopped and listened, but to my surprise I couldn't hear anything. I went to the door and looked inside. There was nobody there!

My heart began to beat violently. What could have happened? 'Laura!' I called. 'Laura!' But only silence answered me.

I went back to the house. The first person I met was Mrs Michelson, the housekeeper.

'Do you know if Lady Glyde has come in yet?' I asked.

'She came in a little while ago,' replied Mrs Michelson. 'I'm afraid, Miss Halcombe, that something very upsetting must have happened. Sir Percival seemed very angry, and Lady Glyde ran upstairs to her room in tears.'

I hurried upstairs at once to Laura's room. She was sitting there alone with her face hidden in her hands. She jumped up with a cry of delight when she saw me.

'What happened, Laura? Did you see Anne?'

'No,' she answered. 'Anne didn't come to the boathouse. She left me this note.' She held out a piece of paper and I read the following words:

I was seen with you yesterday by a fat old man and had to run to save myself. I dare not come back today to meet you, so I'm leaving you this at six in the morning. Try to be patient. I promise you'll see me again soon. AC

'I was just reading the note,' said Laura, 'when a shadow fell across the doorway and Sir Percival came in. He was very angry, and grabbed my arm. Look, here are the marks.'

I saw the most terrible bruises on Laura's soft pale arm. Inside I felt a white-cold anger. How I hated her husband!

'He kept asking what Anne had said to me, and where she was,' said Laura. 'He didn't believe me when I told him I didn't know, and dragged me back to the house.'

'So Anne was right,' I said. 'Someone *did* see you with her yesterday, and that someone was Count Fosco. The Count acted as Sir Percival's spy. He told Sir Percival about your meeting, so Sir Percival was watching and waiting for Anne to come back. Thank goodness she escaped and saved herself.'

'Yes,' said Laura. 'Oh, Marian, I'm so afraid. What will happen to us? If only we could leave this house for ever!'

Chapter 6 Marian Hears Terrible Plans

That night I was sitting alone in my room. It was nearly midnight but I didn't want to go to bed – I wasn't sleepy and there were too many things to think about. The window was wide open and I leaned out to look at the night.

It was dark and quiet, with neither moon nor stars. There was a smell of rain in the still, heavy air, but although the rain was threatening, it hadn't come yet.

I was about to turn away from the window when I smelled a different smell – the smell of tobacco smoke. The next moment I saw two tiny red lights moving across the grass in the blackness. Because the grass was soft there was no sound of footsteps, but I knew the red lights were the cigarettes of Sir Percival and Count Fosco. They often went outside in the evening for a short walk, and on their return would sit smoking together outside the library.

Suddenly I had an idea. I knew that Sir Percival and the Count were having an important conversation – a conversation that probably concerned both Laura's future and mine. I had to find out what they were saying.

There was a narrow veranda running all the way around the roof of the house, with flower pots arranged on it. If I climbed out of my bedroom window, I could creep along the veranda until I reached the part of it directly above the library. There I could kneel down among the flower pots and listen unseen to the conversation below.

It was a dangerous, desperate plan and I would have to be extremely careful. If I knocked a flower pot off the roof, or made

There was a narrow veranda running all the way around the roof of the house, with flower pots arranged on it.

any noise by which I could be discovered, I was afraid to think what Sir Percival would do to me.

I went back inside my room, put on a long black coat and tied a scarf round my hair. This would make it easier for me to slip along the veranda in the darkness without anyone noticing me.

My heart was in my mouth, but at last I found myself directly above the library. Sir Percival and the Count were sitting in their usual chairs, smoking. From my position above them, I heard the Count say, 'We've reached a serious crisis in our affairs, Percival, and we must decide secretly tonight what we're going to do. Let me describe our position, and you tell me if I'm right.

'We both arrived at Blackwater Park desperate for money – you needed thousands of pounds, and I needed hundreds. The simplest and best way for us to get the money was to obtain your wife's signature on a document which would sign over some of her fortune for your immediate use. But because of your bad temper, you failed to do so. So now I want to ask you something. What would happen if your wife died?'

'If she died,' replied Sir Percival, 'her entire fortune of twenty thousand pounds would come to me.'

'I thought so. Do you love your wife, Percival?'

'Why do you ask such a question?'

'Because . . . let's say your wife died before the end of the summer. You would gain twenty thousand pounds and both your money difficulties and mine would be at an end. It's worth thinking about seriously, Percival.'

'Yes, I know,' said Sir Percival slowly. 'Believe me, I *have* thought about it. But there is another difficulty.' He stopped and was silent as if he didn't want to go on.

'Shall I give this other difficulty a name?' asked Count Fosco. 'Could it be called Anne Catherick? But what I don't understand, Percival, is who this woman is and why you're so afraid of her. What hold does she have over you?'

'It's none of your business,' replied Sir Percival rudely.

'Well, then,' said the Count, 'I'm afraid I can't help you if I don't know what the problem is.'

'You *must* help me, Fosco!' There was a desperate note in Sir Percival's voice and he rose to his feet, knocking over his chair. 'The truth is that Anne Catherick knows a terrible secret about me – a secret which, if anybody else found it out, would be the end of me. That's why I shut her up in the asylum, so that nobody would listen to her. Her mother knows the secret too, but she won't say anything to anyone – she's too deeply involved in the matter herself.

'And now Anne Catherick has escaped from the asylum and is somewhere near here. I've done my best to find her – I even went to see her mother – but I've failed. I *must* find her, Fosco! I'm a lost man if I don't.'

There was a silence. Fosco took the lamp and looked hard into Sir Percival's face.

'Yes,' he said at last. 'I see you're telling the truth. All right, I'll help you, Percival, and I won't ask what this terrible secret is that makes you so upset. I'll find out in good time. But tell me something. When I went to the boathouse, there was a strange woman with your wife, but I couldn't see her face. Could it have been Anne Catherick? What does she look like?'

'She looks exactly as my wife would look after a long illness,' replied Sir Percival.

'Extraordinary!' exclaimed the Count in astonishment. 'And yet they are not related at all?'

'No,' replied Sir Percival.

'How very strange. All right, now I know what to look for.'

Not another word was spoken. The two men finished their cigarettes, went back into the library and closed the door.

All I wanted to do was to think about the terrible things I had heard. But suddenly I realized that I was wet through and freezing cold. It had been raining hard for some time and I hadn't even noticed. I made my way slowly and with great difficulty back along the roof to my room, just as a distant clock was striking one o'clock.

But I couldn't sleep all night. I had caught a terrible cold in the cruel rain and when eight o'clock came the next morning, I couldn't get up. My head was aching badly; sometimes I felt an awful coldness and at other times a burning fever.

I knew I was going to be terribly ill. Ill, at such a time!

The story is continued by Mrs Michelson, housekeeper at Blackwater Park

Chapter 7 The Sisters are Separated

When Miss Halcombe became ill so unexpectedly, Sir Percival sent for the doctor straight away. To the alarm of everyone at Blackwater Park, the doctor told us he thought her case was very serious indeed. She lay sick in bed for many days, nursed only by her sister, Lady Glyde, and myself. We took it in turns to sit by her bedside from morning till night.

Count Fosco had to go to London on business, and was away for a week. During his absence, Miss Halcombe's condition didn't improve. The day after his return, I received a message from Sir Percival, saying that he wanted to see me at once in the library. I hurried there, to find Sir Percival and Count Fosco sitting together. Clearly they had been discussing something important, but nothing could have prepared me for Sir Percival's words.

'Mrs Michelson,' he said, 'I want to speak to you about a matter which I decided about some time ago, and which I was going to mention before Miss Halcombe became ill.

'I intend to close up Blackwater Park. It's become too

expensive for me to keep. As soon as Miss Halcombe is well enough to travel, she and Lady Glyde must have a change of air and scene. Count Fosco is going to live in London – he's just bought a house there. I want to sell all my horses except one and get rid of all the servants except you and the gardener. Tell them all that they must leave tomorrow.'

I listened to him in amazement.

'But, Sir Percival, excuse me, I can't dismiss the servants without giving them a month's wages in advance.'

Sir Percival gave me a black look. I was afraid he was going to lose his temper.

'Very well, give them each a month's wages and tell them to go. I will only be here myself for another few weeks.'

A few days later, when the servants had left, I was again sent for by Sir Percival. Again I found Count Fosco sitting with him.

This time Sir Percival had even more astonishing news for me. He wanted me to leave the house at once and travel to Torquay, a small seaside town on the south-west coast of England. He told me he was thinking of sending Lady Glyde and Miss Halcombe there, as the sea air would do them good. I was to look for suitable accommodation for them.

'But who will take care of Miss Halcombe in my absence?'

'Don't worry about that,' said Count Fosco. 'She'll be very well looked after. We've found an excellent woman in the village, Margaret Porcher, who will help Lady Glyde nurse her. In any case, she's beginning to get better again.'

I didn't like the sound of this at all. I knew Margaret Porcher, and had always found her a most unpleasant and unintelligent person. But I had no choice except to do as I was ordered. I left for Torquay that evening.

I was away for three days, during which time I was quite unable to find any suitable accommodation for the two ladies at the price which Sir Percival had told me he would pay. On my return to

Blackwater Park, I found that great changes had taken place. Count Fosco had gone back to London and Lady Glyde had been taken ill too, and had not been out of her room for two days.

I went upstairs at once to see her. She was very pleased to see me, but she was clearly weak and depressed. She was also anxious about Miss Halcombe, as she had heard no news of her sister for two days, so I suggested that we both go to see her at once.

We were stopped in the passage by Sir Percival Glyde.

'Where are you going?' he asked his wife.

'To Marian's room,' she answered.

'You won't find her there,' said Sir Percival. 'Count Fosco has taken her to London with him. She's going to spend a few days there at his house. Margaret Porcher has gone with them to look after her.'

Lady Glyde turned terribly pale, and leaned against the wall, staring at her husband. I was so astonished that I couldn't speak.

'Impossible!' Lady Glyde cried out. 'Marian would never have gone away and left me here by myself.'

'She insisted on going,' replied Sir Percival. 'She plans to go on to Limmeridge House, but she wanted to stay in London for a few days first. She knew you would only start crying and try to stop her if she told you.'

'Then I must follow my sister,' said Lady Glyde. 'I must go where she has gone. I must see that she is alive and well with my own eyes.'

'Why should she not be?' said Sir Percival. 'But yes, you can go. I'll write to Count Fosco today and tell him to expect you by the midday train tomorrow. He'll meet you at the station in London and take you to his house, where you can be reunited with your sister. You can stay there for a few days and then travel on to Limmeridge House together.'

The next day was fine and sunny. At a quarter to twelve, Lady Glyde was ready to leave. She was waiting downstairs for the horse and carriage, when Sir Percival appeared.

He informed her that he had to go out and wouldn't be able to go with her to the station. He asked me to go instead, which I was very glad to do. I felt so sorry for Lady Glyde.

Just as he was about to leave the room, Lady Glyde stopped him at the door and put out her hand.

'I don't think we'll meet again, Percival,' she said. 'This is goodbye for ever. I forgive you for all you have done.'

Sir Percival didn't say a word. Instead, he turned pale and left the room quickly.

The gardener drove us to the station and we arrived just in time for Lady Glyde to catch her train.

'I wish you were coming with me,' she said. 'You have been so kind to Marian and myself and I'll never forget it.'

As the train began to move off, I saw her pale quiet face looking sorrowfully out of the window. She waved her hand, and was gone.

When I returned to Blackwater Park, I went for a walk in the garden. Suddenly I saw a strange woman walking down the path in front of me. As I approached her, she heard my footsteps and turned round.

My blood ran cold with shock. It was Margaret Porcher.

'You! Here!' I cried. 'Not gone to London!'

Her mouth opened wide in a stupid grin, but before she could speak, a man's voice said, 'Certainly not. She's never left Blackwater Park. And neither has Miss Halcombe. She's still here, but we have moved her to a different part of the house, that's all.'

Sir Percival had come up unseen behind me. I stared at him in shock. I couldn't believe what he was saying to me.

'If you don't believe me, come and see her for yourself.'

He led the way to the oldest part of the house. There in a bedroom I saw Miss Halcombe sleeping peacefully. All I could think about was poor Lady Glyde. What would she say, how would she feel, when she got to Count Fosco's house and found her sister wasn't there?

'Sir Percival,' I said, 'you have deceived me and you have deceived your wife cruelly. I don't know why you've done this, but I wish to resign from your service immediately.'

'Very well,' replied Sir Percival, 'but if you go now, there will be nobody left to look after Miss Halcombe. Margaret Porcher is leaving now and I'm leaving tonight.'

As a human being, I knew I couldn't leave Miss Halcombe alone. I knew I had to stay with her until she was better.

That night I saw Sir Percival leave. He jumped on his horse and rode off, his face pale as a ghost in the moonlight.

That was the last time I ever saw Sir Percival Glyde.

The story is continued by Hester Pinhorn, Count Fosco's cook

Chapter 8 A Sudden Death

I'm a cook by profession, and in the summer of 1850 I was looking for a job. I obtained work in the house of Count Fosco, an elderly Italian gentleman who had just bought a house in north London.

A couple of days after I started working for Count Fosco, he told me that a visitor would be arriving the next day. This visitor's name was Lady Glyde. She would be staying with us for a few days before travelling on to her uncle's house in Cumberland, in the north of England.

When Lady Glyde arrived, her appearance gave me quite a shock. The poor lady didn't look at all well. Her face was a most terrible white colour and she looked round all the time with wild staring eyes as if she was very frightened of something. As soon as she entered the house, she fainted. We carried her upstairs and laid her on the bed, then my master sent immediately for the doctor.

The doctor came and examined Lady Glyde carefully. After listening to her heart, he said, 'This is a very serious case indeed. I suggest you write to the lady's friends and relatives at once.'

'Is it heart disease?' asked Count Fosco.

'Yes, and of a most dangerous kind. I'm afraid there isn't much I or any other doctor can do for this poor lady now.'

'Poor Lady Glyde!' said my master, shaking his head. 'Poor dear Lady Glyde!' He seemed terribly upset. He was a strange man – a huge fat old man who kept white mice and spoke to them as if they were children. I liked him because clearly he had a very soft heart.

I sat by the lady's bedside all through the night. She would have been very pretty if she hadn't been so ill – she had lovely fair hair and blue eyes. But she was very weak. She kept sitting up and trying to say something, but I couldn't understand her. I think her mind was very confused and that probably she didn't even know where she was.

The next day she gave a sudden cry and fainted again. When the doctor came, he went upstairs to the bed and bent down over the sick lady. Then he put his hand on her heart.

'I'm afraid it's all over,' he said. 'She's dead. I was afraid this would happen when I examined her yesterday.'

My master, the Count, seemed terribly upset by what had happened. He sat quietly in a corner with his head in his hands, saying nothing.

But there were arrangements to make concerning the funeral and where Lady Glyde was to be buried. First of all, the death had to be recorded and, seeing that Count Fosco was so upset, the doctor offered to do this himself on his way home. The date was 25 July.

Later, my master got in touch with the lady's uncle, a Mr Fairlie who lived in a place called Limmeridge House in Cumberland, and told him the sad news of his niece's death. It was arranged that Lady Glyde's body be sent to Limmeridge and buried in the churchyard there, in the same grave as her mother.

It seemed that the lady's husband was travelling abroad and could not be contacted in time for the funeral. So my master himself went, and very impressive he looked too, all in black, with his huge face, his tall hat and his slow walk.

The story is continued by Walter Hartright

Chapter 9 Back in the Churchyard

Early in the summer of 1850 I and my surviving companions left the wilds and forests of Central America and came home to Britain. I was back in London on the night of 13 October, and went straight away to see my mother.

I had gone to Central America in order to forget the past. I came back a changed man – the dangers I had experienced had made me stronger and more independent. My feelings towards Laura hadn't changed – she was still in all my thoughts. I hadn't forgotten her, but I had learned how to bear the disappointment of losing her to someone else.

But nothing could have prepared me for the shock of hearing about Laura's death. When my mother told me the news, the pain was terrible and I could find no relief. Finally I decided to travel back to Limmeridge and visit Laura's grave. I knew I had to go and see the place where she was buried – where they had laid her to rest. That was the only way I could believe that her death had really happened.

It was a quiet autumn afternoon when the train brought me into the station at Limmeridge. As I walked along the path which led to the small churchyard, the air was warm and still and the countryside lonely but peaceful.

It seemed like only yesterday since I had been here. I kept half expecting that Laura would come down the path to meet me, her summer hat shading her face, her dress blowing in the wind and her sketchbook in her hand.

Soon I arrived at the churchyard. I could see the tall white marble cross over the grave – the grave that now contained both mother and daughter. I remembered that I had once met the Woman in White here. What had happened to her?

I approached the grave. On the white gravestone I saw some newly cut letters. They were black, hard, clear and cruel, and told the story of Laura's life and death.

In memory of Laura, Lady Glyde, wife of Sir Percival Glyde and daughter of the late Philip Fairlie of Limmeridge House. Born March 27th, 1829; married December 22nd, 1849; died July 25th, 1850.

I knelt by the grave, laid my head on the white stone and closed my eyes, thinking about Laura, my lost love.

Time passed. I didn't know how long I'd been kneeling there, but suddenly, I heard a noise, as of someone moving softly over the grass. I looked up. It was nearly sunset and the air was cold and clear.

Two women were standing together in the churchyard. They were looking towards the grave and towards me. They were both wearing veils, so their faces were hidden.

They moved slowly towards me and stopped. One of them raised her veil. In the still evening light, I saw the face of Marian Halcombe.

But how changed she was from the Marian I had known before! How much older she looked! Her eyes had a wild, frightened look and were full of pain and sorrow. She stared at me, looking as if she couldn't believe her eyes.

The woman who was still veiled left her companion and came

towards me slowly and silently. She stopped on one side of the grave. We were standing face to face with the gravestone between us.

The woman lifted her veil.

Laura, Lady Glyde, was standing opposite me, looking at me over her own grave!

PART THREE

Chapter 1 At the Asylum

It is impossible to describe my feelings during the days following the wonderful realization that Laura wasn't dead, but alive. My heart turns when I think about it, and my mind becomes dark and confused. My whole life had been changed and turned in a new direction, and could begin again.

The three of us – Marian, Laura and myself – went to London where we rented rooms in a very poor and crowded part of the city. I wanted to be surrounded by people who were too busy with their own lives to take any notice of us. It was of the greatest importance for us to remain in hiding, and for this purpose we pretended that we were a brother and two sisters. We took different names from our own, and lived as quietly as we could. I earned money for us by selling drawings to cheap newspapers and magazines.

Laura was greatly changed. She was no longer the bright, happy girl I had once known – the experiences she had suffered had caused her beauty to fade and her mind to become clouded.

But although she couldn't remember very much about what had happened to her, she hadn't forgotten the words I said to her when I left Limmeridge House. She repeated them to me in the evening of the day when I found her again: '*Promise me that if ever*

The woman lifted her veil.

a time comes when you need help, you'll remember me – the poor drawing master who taught you. Promise me you'll let me know.'

Now I had the chance to fulfil my promise. The aim of my life was to make things all right again for Laura. I was determined to restore her to her rightful place in society, and to make sure that the two wicked men who had harmed her, Sir Percival and Count Fosco, were punished. I didn't know *how* I was going to do this, but I was going to do it.

Marian told me her story soon after we had been reunited.

'I had lain ill for many days at Blackwater Park,' she said. 'I was too weak and confined to know everything that was going on. But one morning I woke up and discovered that the fever had left me and I was feeling much better, To my surprise, my bed was in a part of the house which I didn't recognize. And the only person who was still at Blackwater Park looking after me was Mrs Michelson, the housekeeper.

'Mrs Michelson told me that my sister, Lady Glyde, had gone to London to stay in Count Fosco's house, and that Sir Percival had also left Blackwater Park, and it was uncertain if he would return. I thought this was all very strange. But then we received some shocking news. I was in the middle of writing a letter to Count Fosco enquiring about Laura, when a letter arrived from him, informing us that she had been taken ill suddenly at his home and had died there.

'On learning this, I became so ill that I couldn't travel for three weeks. Finally I went to London, accompanied by Mrs Michelson who had become a good friend. We parted from each other in London and went our separate ways.

'I went straight away to see our family lawyer, Mr Gilmore. I told him that I was very suspicious of the circumstances in which Laura had died, and I wanted him to find out more about her death and what exactly she had died of. So Mr Gilmore went to Count Fosco's home, where he found the Count very friendly and helpful. He questioned the Count, the cook and the doctor who had seen Laura. Finally he came back to tell me that Laura had died from natural causes – a heart problem. He could find nothing suspicious about her death.

'I then travelled to Limmeridge House to see my uncle, Mr Fairlie. Mr Fairlie told me he had learned about Laura's death in a letter from Count Fosco. The Count had suggested that Laura's body be brought back to the churchyard in Limmeridge and placed in her mother's grave, and Mr Fairlie had agreed to this. The funeral had taken place on 30 July, and Count Fosco had come from London to attend it. Sir Percival Glyde was still travelling abroad.

'A few days after the funeral, Mr Fairlie received another letter from Count Fosco, now back in London.

'Dear Mr Fairlie,
This is to inform you that the woman called Anne Catherick, whom Marian Halcombe can tell you about in detail, was found a few days ago in the area of Sir Percival Glyde's home at Blackwater Park. She has now been taken back to the asylum in north London from which she escaped.
'Unfortunately the mental problems from which she suffered in the past have got worse. She keeps imagining that she is Sir Percival's wife, Lady Glyde. She is doing this to annoy Sir Percival and make him angry. In case she writes to you, telling you she is Lady Glyde, please ignore her letter.
'I remain, sir, your humble servant

Fosco

'Mr Fairlie showed me this letter and asked me about Anne Catherick. When I had explained to him who she was, I decided I would visit her in the asylum where she was being held. I hadn't met her before, but I'd heard about her first from you, Walter, and then from Laura. I'd always been very curious about her, but now I was even more curious because I wanted to know why she was pretending to be my sister.

'Count Fosco's letter didn't give the address of the asylum, but I knew it was in north London and I knew its name because you had told me, Walter, after Anne Catherick herself told you. It was easy to find out where it was, so I travelled there and met with the director. I explained that I was Marian Halcombe, the sister of the late Lady Glyde, and that I wanted to see Anne Catherick, as I understood that Anne thought she was my sister.

'The director had no objections to me seeing Anne Catherick and told me that Anne was at that moment out walking with a nurse in the garden. He took me into the garden himself but was then called back to the asylum on urgent business, leaving me alone there.

'I waited and watched two women coming down a path towards me. One of them was a nurse. The other woman was walking slowly, looking at the ground. When she got nearer, she looked up at me and her eyes met mine. Then she rushed towards me and threw herself into my arms. At that moment, I recognized my sister Laura.

'When I had recovered a little from the shock, I began to think quickly. I knew I had to get Laura out of the asylum as quickly as possible. If I tried to do it by legal means, by explaining to the director that a mistake had been made, it would take too long. I had to act now. I whispered to Laura that I would come back for her the next day, and asked the nurse if I could meet her alone the next morning.

'I had a few hundred pounds in my bank, and I went straight back to London and took this money out. Then I returned to the asylum. I showed the nurse the money and told her I would give it to her if she helped Laura escape. At last the nurse agreed. She told me to wait. Just over an hour later, she returned, leading Laura by the arm. I handed over the money and took Laura back to London by the afternoon train.

'I found my poor sister sadly changed. She knew me, but her

memory was confused and very weak. I tried to ask her what had happened, but she could remember very little.

'I thought the best thing would be to take her back to her old home at Limmeridge House. So the following day, we took the train to Limmeridge.'

Chapter 2 Walter Makes a Plan of Action

When I gently asked Laura if she could remember anything about what had happened to her, she replied, 'When I took the train from Blackwater Park to London, Count Fosco was waiting on the platform in London to meet me. The train was very crowded and it was very difficult to find my luggage, but in the end Count Fosco got it and took me outside to his carriage. We got in and drove away.

'I asked at once about Marian. Count Fosco told me that she was waiting at his house for me and that I would see her very soon, and not to worry.

'I don't know London very well, and it was quite impossible for me to recognize any of the streets which we drove through. At last we stopped in a small street behind a square. I remember that in this square there were shops and many people – it didn't look like the kind of area where people had their homes. However, I asked the Count if this was where he lived and he told me it was.'

'I'm quite sure it wasn't his real house,' I said. 'I think he took you somewhere else. What happened next?'

'We got out of the carriage and went inside. A servant came and took my luggage and showed me the way upstairs. Again I asked Count Fosco about Marian and again he promised that I'd see her soon. He said he'd go and tell her I'd arrived.

'A few minutes later he came back, looking worried, and told me that Marian was still sleeping and that I couldn't see her yet.

He then said that Marian had become ill again that morning. On hearing this news, I began to feel faint and asked if I could have a drink. The room was terribly hot. The Count called a servant and told him to bring some tea.

'A few minutes later the tea arrived and the Count poured me a cup. It tasted rather strange, and as I was drinking it, my head started to spin. I remember falling to the floor, and the Count catching my cup as it dropped out of my hand. Then everything went black.

'From then on, I remember nothing at all. I don't know how much time passed before I woke up. But when I woke I was in a strange place, surrounded by women I didn't know. And I was wearing somebody else's clothes.'

'That strange place was the asylum,' I said. 'Count Fosco must have put something in your tea to send you to sleep.'

'In the place where I was, people were calling me Anne Catherick,' continued Laura. 'I couldn't understand it. There were nurses around – they weren't unkind to me, but they kept telling me to stop pretending I was Lady Glyde. They told me Lady Glyde was dead and buried, and to look at my clothes, which had Anne Catherick's name on.'

'And so they did,' said Marian. 'When I got Laura back to London, and looked at her clothes, everything was marked with Anne Catherick's name.'

'After Sir Percival and Count Fosco had found Anne Catherick again,' I said, 'Count Fosco must have brought her to London and kept her in his house. She was very ill and he knew she would die. After her death, he must have brought her clothes with him when he met Laura, and when Laura fell asleep, put them on her. Meanwhile, he took Laura's clothes and dressed Anne Catherick's body in them.'

'It was a very clever plan,' said Marian. 'I'm sure it was the Count's idea – Sir Percival isn't clever enough to think of a plan like that. And the one thing that made it possible was the extraordinary likeness between Anne Catherick and Laura.'

'What happened when you took Laura to Limmeridge House?' I asked Marian. 'What did your uncle say?'

'It was terrible,' replied Marian. 'I had been absolutely sure that my uncle would welcome Laura back to Limmeridge House and give her a home again there. But to my great astonishment and anger, he refused to recognize her. He kept insisting that Laura was really Anne Catherick pretending to be Laura. He told me that I was a fool to believe her.

'He angrily reminded me about Count Fosco's letter, warning him about Anne Catherick, and that I myself had told him how much Laura and Anne Catherick looked like each other. Even when I brought Laura to his room, he insisted that he didn't recognize her, and said that Laura lay buried in the churchyard at Limmeridge. Finally he said that if I didn't take this madwoman away at once, he would call the police, as all he wanted was to be left alone in peace and quiet.

'Of course I was very shocked and disappointed at my uncle's behaviour, but when I took Laura to meet the servants, it wasn't much better. None of them recognized her for sure. The sad truth was that her looks had changed so much because of her terrible experiences that she didn't look at all like the happy girl whom they had known before. She looked pale and thin, and just a shadow of her old self. I remembered how Sir Percival had told Count Fosco that Anne Catherick looked exactly like Laura after a long illness.

'I knew it was dangerous to stay longer at Limmeridge House, if Mr Fairlie wasn't going to give us any help or support. I was afraid that people from the asylum would come to Limmeridge looking for the woman they said was Anne Catherick, and that Mr Fairlie would hand Laura straight back to them. So I knew we had to leave Limmeridge at once, and I decided the safest place for us to be was London. As we walked to the station to catch the afternoon train, Laura insisted on seeing our mother's grave for the last time, so we walked by the churchyard. That was where we met you, and the rest you know!'

Having heard the stories of both Marian and Laura, two things became very clear to me. First, it was clear that Sir Percival and Count Fosco had found the real Anne Catherick, and seeing that she was weak and ill, Count Fosco had taken her to his home and introduced her there as Lady Glyde. Meanwhile, Laura had been handed over to the asylum as Anne Catherick. It had all been managed very cleverly, so that nobody – Count Fosco's cook, the doctor who saw Anne, the director of the asylum or the nurses there – had been in any way suspicious.

Second, I knew very well that if Sir Percival or the Count found us, we could expect no mercy from them. They had gained twenty thousand pounds by their cruel trick of deceiving everyone into thinking that Laura was dead, and naturally they wouldn't want to give up this money. Now that Laura had escaped from the asylum, they would do everything in their power to pursue her, and if they found her, they would take her away from us. We were all in great danger from them, but especially Laura.

We lived as quietly as we could, therefore, in this poor crowded part of London, taking no notice of anybody and hoping that we too were unnoticed. Every day I went out to work while Marian and Laura stayed at home, and never opened the door to anyone. Marian looked after the house and did all the work herself, so no strangers had to come there.

Meanwhile, I was deciding on a plan of action.

Chapter 3 Mrs Catherick Shares a Secret

More than anything else, I wanted to punish Sir Percival Glyde for what he had done to Laura, the woman I loved. I wanted to punish Count Fosco too, but it was Sir Percival whom I hated the most. As

Laura's husband, he had treated her very cruelly, then he had caused everyone to believe that she was dead, and had shut her up in the asylum while taking her fortune of twenty thousand pounds.

Anne Catherick had told me that she knew a deep dark secret about Sir Percival which would destroy him if anyone found it out. We knew that this secret existed, but we had failed to learn the details of it from Anne. However, Anne had told Laura there was one other person who knew it – her mother, Mrs Catherick.

I therefore made up my mind to go and visit Mrs Catherick. The housekeeper at Blackwater Park had told Marian that she lived in the village of Welmingham, about twenty miles away from Sir Percival's house, so I took the train there. I didn't know Mrs Catherick's house, but by asking the local people, I was soon able to find out where she lived, in a small untidy house overlooking a square.

The door was opened by an unsmiling servant. I gave the servant my card and a few minutes later was told that Mrs Catherick would see me. I was shown into a room where an elderly woman, dressed in black, was sitting upright in a chair by the window. This was Mrs Catherick.

Immediately I noticed the expression on her face. It was very hard and cold. Her dark eyes looked straight ahead, and the first words she spoke were not words of welcome.

'Who are you and what do you want?' she asked.

'My name is Walter Hartright,' I replied, 'and I've come to tell you about your daughter, Anne. You knew that she was lost, but now I'm afraid I have to tell you some very sad news – I'm afraid that Anne is dead.'

To my astonishment, Mrs Catherick didn't show any emotion or sadness at all. She didn't seem upset in any way by the news that her only daughter was dead. All she said was, 'Why have you come to tell me this? What possible concern is it of yours? Why are you so interested?'

'Your daughter's death . . .' I began.

'What did she die of?'

'Of heart disease.'

'Oh, yes, it's true her heart was very weak. Go on.'

'Two men have played a part in your daughter's death,' I said, 'and have used it to bring harm to another person, a lady whom I love dearly. That's why I'm interested. I want to make sure these two wicked men are properly punished. The name of one of them is Sir Percival Glyde.'

If I had expected Mrs Catherick to show some feeling when she heard Sir Percival's name, I was disappointed. Her face remained as cold and expressionless as a stone.

'Mrs Catherick,' I said, 'I'll speak openly with you. I know that you know something about Sir Percival Glyde – some kind of secret from his past that will destroy him if it becomes known. Please tell me what this secret is.'

Mrs Catherick's lips parted in a thin cruel smile.

'I'll tell you nothing,' she said. 'It's none of your business.'

'At first,' I went on, 'I thought Sir Percival's secret might be that he had had a relationship with you. I thought he might have been your lover and Anne's father. But now I don't think so – the secret between you and Sir Percival is not that. It goes much deeper and is something quite different, isn't it?'

Mrs Catherick got up from her chair and came up close to me with a look of great anger.

'How dare you talk to me about Anne's father!' she exclaimed. 'How dare you say who her father was or wasn't! Go! Leave my house at once!'

'Are you afraid of Sir Percival?' I asked.

'Afraid? Why should I be afraid of him?'

'Because he has a high position in society. Because he's a rich and powerful man who owns a lot of land. Because he's a baronet, of very good family.'

Mrs Catherick stared at me in astonishment. Then she surprised me by beginning to laugh. She laughed so much that she couldn't stop. At last she said, 'Of very good family? A baronet? Yes, indeed, a *very* great family, especially on the mother's side.'

'Whatever do you mean?' I asked.

'Go to the church near Blackwater Park and look at the book that contains the records of all the marriages that have taken place in the district. Look at the entry that records the marriage of Sir Percival Glyde's parents. Then come back to me and tell me if you still think he is a baronet of very good family.'

I looked at her in silence for a moment. Then I said, 'Very well. I'll go to the church. But I'll be back.'

Chapter 4 The Proof of the Crime

I left the house, feeling that Mrs Catherick had helped me in spite of herself. At least I had a new clue and a new direction to follow.

I took the train to Blackwater Park and walked to the local church. On the way, I thought about Anne Catherick. Poor Anne! She must have spent many sad and lonely years with her mother. Clearly Mrs Catherick was a cruel, hard woman, who had had no love or tender feelings for her daughter.

But why had she got so angry when I asked about Anne's father? If her father wasn't Sir Percival Glyde, who was he?

The church was about two miles from the station and stood by itself on a high point of ground. Not far away I noticed a row of cottages, and knocked at the door of the first one I came to. I was looking for the clerk of the church, the man responsible for looking after the documents relating to church business. I hoped he would be able to show me where all the marriage records were kept.

The clerk came out, and I explained to him what I wanted. He listened, then went back inside his cottage and came out carrying a rusty old key. He explained that this was the key to the vestry, the small room adjoining the church where boxes of important papers and other documents were kept.

The clerk and I walked up to the church together. The vestry had a separate entrance from the rest of the church. The clerk put the key in the lock, and after twisting and turning it, managed to open the door with great difficulty. He explained that the lock had needed changing for a long time, but that nothing had been done about it.

It was very dark and dusty inside the vestry, and the air smelled damp and heavy. A number of packing boxes and papers were lying about the floor and the whole place was very untidy. The clerk opened a cupboard and took out an enormous book with a leather cover. This was the book where all the marriages in the district had been recorded.

I knew Sir Percival's age – about forty-five – so I could work out the approximate date when his parents got married. I started with the year 1803. There, in September of that year, I found the entry which recorded his parents' marriage. It showed the marriage of Sir Felix Glyde to a lady called Cecilia Jane Elster.

All the other entries on the page had been written very clearly, in large handwriting. But this one was different. The entry appeared in tiny handwriting, in a tiny space right at the bottom of the page.

It was almost as if someone had added it to the book later.

I looked very carefully at the handwriting in which the entry was written. There was something about it which was very familiar to me. I knew I had seen it somewhere before. But where?

Suddenly I realized the truth. I *had* seen the handwriting before – in letters from Sir Percival which Marian had shown me at Limmeridge House. Sir Percival had entered the marriage of his parents into the book himself. The entry which recorded the marriage of his parents was a forgery – it was a lie and completely false!

If it was a forgery, where was the original entry? Could it be that there *was* no original entry – that Sir Percival Glyde's parents had never actually been married?

My heart gave a great leap. If this were true, then I knew Sir Percival's secret. If he was the child of a couple who never married, then Sir Percival Glyde wasn't Sir Percival Glyde at all. He wasn't a baronet and had no legal rights to Blackwater Park. It could all be taken from him. Moreover, forgery was a serious crime and I knew that the punishment was very severe. He could be sent to prison for a very long time. No wonder he didn't want to be found out!

I handed the book back to the clerk, thanked him, and caught the next train back to Welmingham. I went straight to Mrs Catherick's house and pushed my way through the door to find her still sitting in the same chair. She could see at once by my face that I had found out the truth.

'So you know Sir Percival's secret,' she said. 'Yes, it's true. Well, maybe it's a good thing you've found it out. Perhaps it's time it was discovered.'

'But how did you get involved?' I asked.

'I used to live near Blackwater Park,' she said, 'and I had a job cleaning the church there. One morning in the year 1827 I got to the church earlier than usual. A gentleman was in the vestry, writing something in the book where marriages are recorded. When he turned round, I recognized Sir Percival Glyde.

'Sir Percival had only recently come back to England to live at Blackwater Park. He had been born and brought up abroad, but his parents had both died suddenly, and he had returned.

'When he knew I had seen him, he became very frightened. He begged me not to tell anyone what he had done, and promised to bring me lovely presents from London. He gave me beautiful dresses and watches.

'I didn't know that forgery was a serious crime so I accepted his presents. And by doing so, I made myself an accomplice to his crime. Now if I told anyone about him, I would be in terrible trouble as well. So I kept quiet for many years, and went on accepting his presents.

'But one day, my daughter Anne heard me talking to myself about it. The next time she saw Sir Percival, she told him she knew his secret. I don't think she understood it properly but Sir Percival was frightened and he immediately shut her up in the asylum. To tell the truth, I didn't really mind, because she was very weak in the head and she was always a trouble to me, so I agreed to let him do it.'

'Thank you, Mrs Catherick,' I said quietly when she had finished. 'You have helped me greatly. I now have the information I need to destroy Sir Percival Glyde.'

Mrs Catherick smiled one of her thin cruel smiles.

'No, you don't,' she said. 'You can't prove a thing. The proof of the crime is in the book which you left in the vestry of the church.'

'Then,' I said, 'I'll go back to the church to get it.'

'You'd better hurry,' said Mrs Catherick. 'I've sent my servant to Blackwater Park to warn Sir Percival Glyde about what you're doing. Sir Percival returned there yesterday.'

Chapter 5 A Second Death

It was dark when I got back to the church. I came to the path which ran by the clerk's cottage and saw a light in his window. I went up the path to the front door, intending to ask the clerk for the key to the vestry.

Before I could knock on the door, it opened and a man came running out with a lighted lantern in his hand. I stared at him in great surprise − it was the clerk, but looking very different from how he had appeared that morning. His cheeks were very red, and he appeared suspicious and confused. His first words to me astonished me.

'Where are the keys?' he asked. 'Have you taken them?'

'What keys?' I asked.

'The keys of the vestry. What shall I do? The keys are gone! Do you hear? The keys are gone!'

'How? When? Who could have taken them?'

'I don't know,' said the clerk. 'I closed my window this morning, but someone got inside my house and took the keys.'

'Get another light,' I said, 'and let's go to the vestry together. Hurry! It's not too late to catch this person, whoever he is.'

The clerk went back inside. While I was waiting for him, I suddenly heard someone coming towards me along the path, but the darkness made it impossible to see his face.

'Sir Percival . . .' said a man's voice.

'I'm not Sir Percival,' I replied. 'Did you expect to meet him here?'

'Sir Percival is my master,' said the man. 'He told me to wait for him here while he went into the church.'

So Sir Percival was in the church! I knew what he had come for − to steal or destroy the book which contained his forgery, so that I could not use it as proof of his crime. The clerk came out of his cottage with another lantern, and I took his arm and hurried him up the path to the church. Sir Percival's servant followed close behind us.

As we got to the end of the path, we met a small child.

'Please, sir,' said the child, 'there's someone in the church. I heard him lock the door, and strike a light with a match.'

We turned the corner at the top of the path and saw the church before us. But then we had a terrible shock.

There was a very bright light shining from inside the vestry. As we got near, we could smell a strange smell on the night air − it was smoke! The light inside the vestry was getting brighter and brighter, and at the same time we heard a crackling noise. The vestry was on fire!

I ran to the vestry door and stopped as I heard something which filled me with horror. Someone was desperately trying to open the door from the other side and I could hear a man's voice, screaming for help.

'Oh, my God,' shouted the servant. 'It's Sir Percival.'

'God have mercy on him,' cried the clerk. 'He's locked himself in and the lock has broken. He can't get out!'

I rushed to the door. I completely forgot that Sir Percival was my enemy and all the wicked things he had done. All I could think of was that we had to save him from a horrible death. He was a human being, after all.

I could hear no sound from within to show that he was still alive. All I could hear was the crackling noise of the flames. Without thinking of my own safety I climbed up on to the roof of the vestry where there was a small glass window. I broke it with my stick, and the flames shot up into the night sky. But I couldn't see Sir Percival.

Meanwhile the villagers had seen the fire and had begun to gather outside the church.

'Call the fire engine!' somebody shouted. 'Let's try to save the church!'

I climbed down from the roof with the idea of breaking down the door of the vestry from the outside. I took two men and rushed down the path which led back to the clerk's cottage. There we found a long piece of wood which we brought back to the church and threw against the door of the vestry. At last the door fell in with a crash, but we were prevented from going inside by a sheet of living flames.

At that moment the fire engine arrived and the firemen ran to the vestry and directed water inside. As the water fell on to the

At last the door fell in with a crash, but Walter and the two men were prevented from going inside by a sheet of living flames.

flames, the fire gradually died down and went out.

A man's body, blackened and burned, was found lying face down on the floor of the vestry. An old door was brought from the village and the body was placed on it, carried outside and put down on the grass. Someone put a cloth over it and the people crowded round.

'Where is the gentleman who tried to save him?' the chief fireman said.

I felt many hands pushing me forwards.

'Here I am,' I said. I was pushed into the middle of a small circle with the body lying at my feet.

'Can you tell us who he is, sir?'

I looked down slowly. The silence was terrible as I pulled back the cloth which covered the body. There, black and terrible in the yellow light of the lanterns, was the dead burned face of the man who had been Laura's husband.

I told the people I had never seen the man before, but then a voice behind me spoke. It was Sir Percival's servant.

'That's my master,' he said. 'That's Sir Percival Glyde.'

Chapter 6 Walter is Rewarded

The next day there was an official enquiry into what had taken place in the vestry of the church – what Sir Percival was doing there and how he had met his death.

The clerk told the court how his keys had disappeared from his house. The enquiry came to the conclusion that Sir Percival had locked himself in the vestry, not knowing that the lock was broken and it would be very difficult to get out again. The fire in the vestry had started by accident. Maybe he knocked his lantern over, which contained a lot of oil and so would quickly start a fire. Moreover, there were many dry materials in the vestry –

papers and old boxes – which would burn quickly and cause a fire to spread easily.

But the enquiry couldn't find a reason for Sir Percival being in the vestry or why he had locked himself in there. Everything in the vestry had been burned with him, including the book of marriage records and other important documents.

I knew very well what Sir Percival had been doing in the vestry, but I wasn't going to say anything. He was looking for the book of marriage records, intending either to steal it or to tear out the page with the false marriage entry. While he was looking for it, he locked the door so that nobody would disturb him. He was probably in a great hurry and knocked over his lantern in the darkness by accident.

The enquiry reached the conclusion that the cause of Sir Percival Glyde's death was death by sudden accident.

When everything was finished, I walked through the village back to the small hotel where I had stayed the night before. I passed the square where Mrs Catherick lived, and thought about going in to see her. Then I decided not to. I had nothing really to say to her, and I was sure she would already have heard about Sir Percival's death.

However, as I was packing my things at the hotel, to my surprise I received a note from Mrs Catherick.

Dear Mr Hartright

I watched you walk by my house this morning. Why didn't you call in and see me? I have heard the news about Sir Percival. You frightened him with your enquiries, and caused him to bring about his own downfall, and I'm grateful to you for that. I heard you tried to save him. Why? I'm glad you didn't succeed.

You found out many things from me, including Sir Percival's secret. But there is something you still don't know, and because I know you will be interested, I'll tell you. Think of it as a kind of reward to you from me.

You wanted to know who Anne's father was but you couldn't guess the truth. During the summer of 1826, I was a maid in service at a large house belonging to a gentleman called Major Donthorne. Major Donthorne had a very good friend who came to stay with him. The name of the Major's friend was Mr Philip Fairlie and he had a house in the north of England, near a village called Limmeridge.

In those days I was a pretty girl, and I soon caught Mr Philip Fairlie's eye. He was one of the most handsome and best men in England. We had a relationship, and after he left I found I was going to have a child.

There was a local man who loved me called John Catherick. I didn't love him, but because of what had happened I agreed to marry him. When my baby was born – a little girl whom I called Anne – everyone, including my husband, thought that the child was his and nobody asked any questions about it.

I never told Mr Fairlie about his daughter because I knew he was already married. Now do you understand?
Yours sincerely

Jane Catherick

I sat and thought about the letter for a long time. I *did* understand. Everything was very clear to me and the mystery was solved at last. The shocking truth was that Laura and Anne had had the same father. That was why they looked so like each other – they were half-sisters.

Chapter 7 The End of the Affair

That evening I returned home to London, where Marian and Laura were waiting for me. It was wonderful to be all together again. Later, after Laura was in bed, I told Marian the whole story of how Sir Percival had met his death, and the information I had learned from Mrs Catherick about Anne's father. We decided that it would be best for Laura not to know any of the details of this until she was stronger; we would tell her only that her husband was dead.

Every day Laura was becoming brighter, and it gave me enormous pleasure to see how much better she was. She sometimes looked and spoke just like the Laura of old times, the happy girl whom I had first met at Limmeridge House.

When we were alone together, my heart would beat quickly just like in the old days, and my hands would tremble. I noticed too how happy she was when she was with me, how her clear eyes shone and the colour came into her cheeks. I loved her just as much as ever, but I hesitated to ask her to become my wife. She was so friendless, so helpless.

Yet I knew the situation couldn't go on as it was. I had to speak to Laura and know what my future was with her, one way or the other. So I asked Marian for her advice.

'My dear Walter,' replied Marian, 'I was responsible for separating you from Laura and sending you away once before, and that was my greatest mistake. This time I'm going to do no such thing. Tell her freely what's in your heart.'

So I spoke to Laura, and asked her to marry me. To my great joy and delight, she agreed to be my wife. We were married ten days later, and I had never experienced such happiness.

Meanwhile, what of Count Fosco? I learned that he had sold his house in north London and gone to live abroad. I thought long and hard about pursuing him, but in the end I decided to let him go. My main enemy had been Sir Percival Glyde and Sir Percival was now dead. Also, now that I had married Laura, my position had changed and I saw things differently from the way I had when I was single. I didn't want to do anything which would risk destroying our new-found happiness. We had waited a long time to be together and had overcome many difficulties. I didn't want to do anything which would take our happiness away or bring danger to her life or mine.

Mr Fairlie rose from his chair, supported on each side by a strong servant holding his arm.

Years later, we heard that Count Fosco had died in Paris.

When Laura was strong again, I took her to see Mr Gilmore, the family lawyer. Mr Gilmore was quite amazed, and listened with astonishment to my story of what had happened. He immediately wrote to Laura's uncle, Mr Fairlie of Limmeridge House, informing him that his niece was most certainly alive and would be coming to visit him soon. In the letter, he asked Mr Fairlie to call together all the servants in the house and all the people from the village to meet Laura.

We travelled to Limmeridge House and walked into the main room where a great crowd of people was waiting to see us. A gasp of surprise went up when Laura walked through the door, looking just the same as she used to in the days before her marriage to Sir Percival Glyde.

Mr Fairlie rose from his chair, supported on each side by a strong servant holding his arm.

'May I present Mr Hartright and his wife,' he said to the people. 'Please hear what he has to say and don't make a noise. My nerves are very delicate, you know.'

With these words, Mr Fairlie sank back down again into his chair. I told the people what had happened – that a terrible mistake had been made and another woman, Anne Catherick, lay dead and buried in the churchyard at Limmeridge and not Laura. I told them about Sir Percival Glyde and the wicked things he had done to obtain Laura's fortune.

When I'd finished speaking, there was silence for a moment, then everyone began to cheer. I asked them all to follow me to the churchyard, and see the letters which recorded Laura's death removed from the gravestone.

The villagers crowded round the grave. A man with a hammer came forward and began to remove the black letters which told of Laura's life and death. Later, some other letters were put on the gravestone. They simply said, *Anne Catherick, died July 25th, 1850.*

Then we returned to London and the following year our first child, a little boy, was born. We called him Walter.

One day, when Walter was about six months old, I had to go to Ireland on business. When I returned to London, to my great surprise, I found our house empty and only a short note from Marian left for me. The note said that she, Laura and little Walter had all gone to Limmeridge House, and that I wasn't to worry about anything, but was to follow them there as soon as possible.

I couldn't imagine what had happened. When I arrived at Limmeridge House, there was no sign of Mr Fairlie. I found Marian and Laura sitting comfortably together in the small sitting room where I used to do my work.

'What's happened?' I asked. 'Where's Mr Fairlie?'

Marian then told me that Mr Fairlie had died of a heart attack, that Mr Gilmore had informed them of his death and advised them to go to Limmeridge House immediately. On her uncle's death, Limmeridge House now belonged to Laura.

Bright tears of happiness were shining in Marian's eyes.

'Do you know who this is?' she said, holding up my son.

'What do you mean?' I replied. 'He's my child.'

'Yes,' said Marian, laughing, 'he's your child, but he's also a Very Important Person. Let me introduce you. You are looking at the future owner of Limmeridge House.'

And that was how our story ended, with these words from Marian, the good angel of all our lives.

ACTIVITIES

Part One: Chapters 1–3

Before you read

1 Look at the Word List at the back of the book. Answer these questions with words from the Word List.
   a Which words describe things you do with your mouth?
   b Which words describe things that people wear?
   c Which words are names for a type of person or being?
   d Which words describe a place?

2 Read the Introduction and answer these questions.
   a Who is the Woman in White?
   b What is Wilkie Collins famous for?
   c Which are his two most famous novels and when were they published?
   d Which two men in the story are described as evil?

While you read

3 Underline the wrong word(s) in each sentence and write the right word.
   a Walter Hartright teaches French.   ....
   b Walter is going to work at a place called
      Hampstead Heath.   ....
   c The Woman in White wants to go to
      Cumberland.   ....
   d Marian Halcombe is Laura Fairlie's sister.   ....
   e Mr Fairlie is interested in talking to Walter.   ....
   f Marian looks like the Woman in White.   ....
   g Walter falls in love with Marian.   ....
   h Laura is going to marry Sir Percival Gilmore.   ....
   i The letter to Laura says that Sir Percival is
      a good man.   ....

After you read

4 Answer these questions.

   a Why is Walter so surprised by the Woman in White?

   b Why does Walter think it is possible that the Woman in White's name is Anne Catherick?

   c Why does Marian tell Walter he must leave Limmeridge House?

   d What do we learn about Laura's marriage?

   e Why is Laura so upset by the letter?

5 Discuss these questions.

   a Why do you think The Woman in White is alone on Hampstead Heath at night?

   b Why do you think Laura Fairlie and The Woman in White look like each other?

   c Why does Walter think that the letter to Laura is from the Woman in White?

Part One: Chapters 4–6

Before you read

6 Answer the questions.

   a What do you think Laura, Marian and Walter will do about the letter from The Woman in White?

   b Do you think Laura will marry Sir Percival Glyde?

While you read

7 Put these sentences in the right order, from 1–7.

   a Mr Gilmore says he will send a copy of the letter to Sir Percival Glyde. .....

   b Mr Fairlie writes a note to Walter. .....

   c Laura plays the piano. .....

   d Walter and Marian discover that Anne Catherick has left the farm where she was staying. .....

   e Walter and Marian visit the village school. .....

   f Walter realizes that Laura loves him. .....

   g Walter talks to Anne Catherick by Mrs Fairlie's grave. .....

After you read

8 Who says these things? Who to? Explain the situation.

    a 'It was the ghost of a woman, dressed all in white.'

    b 'I've run away and I'm not going back.'

    c 'I'll write to our family lawyer Mr Gilmore and tell him what happened.'

    d 'I am really very disappointed in you.'

    e 'She was taken ill after that.'

    f 'Now I want to tell you that I'll take over the matter.'

    g 'It's better this way. It's better for you and for her.'

    h 'For God's sake, leave me!'

9 Describe the characters of these people in one or two sentences.

    a The Woman in White   **b** Marian   **c** Mr Fairlie

10 Do you think Mr Gilmore is right to send the letter to Sir Percival Glyde and ask for an explanation?

Part One: Chapters 7–9

Before you read

11 Answer the questions.

    a What do you think Sir Percival Glyde's explanation will be regarding Anne Catherick's letter?

    b What do you think will happen regarding Laura's marriage to Sir Percival Glyde?

While you read

12 Are these sentences right (✓) or wrong (✗)?

    a The story is continued by Mr Gilmore.   .....

    b Mr Gilmore dislikes Sir Percival.   .....

    c Sir Percival explains that Anne Catherick had a physical illness.   .....

    d Mrs Catherick confirms Sir Percival's explanation.   .....

    e Laura will receive £30,000 on her twenty-first birthday.   .....

    f Sir Percival insists that if Laura dies without children, all her money must go to him.   .....

g Mr Fairlie agrees to the marriage settlement because
he likes Sir Percival. .....

h Mr Gilmore continues the story. .....

i Laura is no longer in love with Walter. .....

j Laura and Sir Percival marry on 22nd December. .....

After you read

13 Complete these sentences.

    a Sir Percival's explanation regarding Anne Catherick is that ...

    b Anne Catherick hates Sir Percival because ...

    c If Laura dies before Sir Percival, she wants her money ...

    d Mr Fairlie agrees to Sir Percival's demands because ...

    e Marian helps Walter by ...

    f Mr Fairlie upsets Laura by ...

    g After the wedding, Sir Percival's plan is to ...

14 Work with another student. Have this conversation.

    Student A: You are Laura. Talk about your feelings about Walter
and Sir Percival, and your reasons for marrying Sir
Percival.

    Student B: You are Marian. Explain why you feel anxious about
Laura's marriage. Try to persuade her not to do it.

15 What do you think of the behaviour of these people.

    a Laura **b** Marian **c** Mr Gilmore **d** Sir Percival

Part Two: Chapters 1–4

Before you read

16 Which of these things do you think will happen?

    a Laura will be unhappy in her marriage.

    b Anne Catherick will return.

    c Sir Percival will try to take Laura's money.

    d Sir Percival will try to kill Laura.

    e Walter will return and persuade Laura to run away with him.

    f Laura will die.

17 Complete these sentences with one or two words.

    a Marian, Sir Percival, Laura and Count Fosco arrive at Blackwater Park .... months later.

    b Marian discovers that .... has visited Blackwater Park.

    c Sir Percival is now .... to Laura.

    d Mr Merriman is Sir Percival's ....

    e Sir Percival needs Laura to give him her ....

    f Sir Percival asks Laura to .... a document.

    g Laura and Marian see a .... by the lake.

    h Laura meets .... in the boathouse.

    i Anne Catherick tells Laura that she knows something that will .... Sir Percival.

After you read

18 Answer these questions.

    a How does Marian learn that Mrs Catherick has been to Blackwater Park?

    b What does Marian think is strange about Mrs Catherick's visit?

    c Who is Mr Merriman and what does he tell Sir Percival?

    d What is Laura's reaction to Sir Percival's demand?

    e What are the circumstances that cause Laura and Anne Catherick to meet?

    f Why doesn't Anne Catherick tell Laura what she knows?

    g What do they agree to do?

19 Describe:

    a Laura's feelings and behaviour towards Sir Percival.

    b the reasons for Marian's sense of guilt.

    c Count Fosco.

20 Discuss these questions.

    a What do you think Sir Percival's dark secret might be?

Part Two: Chapters 5–9

Before you read

21 Answer these questions.

    a Do you think Laura will sign the document? If she doesn't, what do you think will happen?

    b Do you think Sir Percival will find Anne? If he does, what do you think will happen?

While you read

22 Put these sentences in the right order, from 1–8.

    a Marian becomes very ill.   .....

    b Walter is very surprised to meet two women.   .....

    c Mrs Michelson discovers that Marian has not left Blackwater Park.   .....

    d Anne Catherick leaves a note for Laura.   .....

    e Marian learns that Count Fosco has been for a walk.   .....

    f Laura dies.   .....

    g Marian listens to the conversation between Sir Percival and Count Fosco.   .....

    h Laura goes to London.   .....

After you read

23 Explain the importance of the following in the story.

    a Anne Catherick's note

    b The conversation between Sir Percival and Count Fosco in the library

    c Marian's illness

    d Walter's return

24 Describe the role of Count Fosco in London.

25 Describe your feelings as you read these chapters, giving reasons for them.

Part Three: Chapters 1–3

Before you read

26 What explanation can there be for Laura's presence at her own grave?

While you read

27 Who:

a lives in London with Marian and Laura? ....

b does Marian visit after she learns about
Laura's death? ....

c does Anne Catherick now claim she is,
according to Sir Percival? ....

d rescues Laura from the asylum? ....

e doesn't let Laura see Marian? ....

f drugs Laura? ....

g refuses to recognize Laura? ....

h visits Mrs Catherick? ....

i tells Walter to visit a church? ....

After you read

28 Explain the situation behind these words.

a Laura was greatly changed.

b On learning this, I became so ill that I couldn't travel for three weeks.

c She is doing this to annoy Sir Percival and make him angry.

d At last the nurse agreed.

e And I was wearing somebody else's clothes.

f I knew it was dangerous to stay longer at Limmeridge House.

29 Work with another student. Using your own words, act out the conversation between Walter and Mrs Catherick.

30 Who do you admire most in these chapters? Who do you dislike most? Give your reasons.

Part Three: Chapters 4–7

Before you read

31 What do you think Walter will discover in the church?

32 Look at the chapter titles. How do you think the story will end?

While you read

33 Are these sentences right (✓) or wrong (✗)?

    a Walter discovers that Sir Percival's parents were not
       married.   .....

    b The church clerk warns Sir Percival that Walter knows
       his secret.   .....

    c Sir Percival dies in a fire in the church.   .....

    d The clerk climbs on the church roof to try and rescue
       Sir Percival.   .....

    e The enquiry decides that Sir Percival killed himself.   .....

    f Anne Catherick's father was Mr Frederick Fairlie.   .....

    g Laura and Walter marry at Limmeridge House.   .....

    h Limmeridge House now belongs to Laura.   .....

After you read

34 Answer these questions.

    a How does Sir Percival die and why?

    b What does Walter do to try and save Sir Percival?

    c What happens to Count Fosco after Sir Percival's death?

    d How does the story end for Walter, Laura and Marian?

35 Describe Mrs Catherick's role in the story from Walter's point of view.

36 Answer these questions. Give reasons for your answer.

    a How do you feel about Sir Percival's death?

    b What is your opinion about the role of Mrs Catherick?

    c Does the ending satisfy you?

Writing

37 Explain how Walter and Marian act as detectives in the novel. Who do you think contributes more to the story, Walter or Marian?

38 Imagine you are Marian Halcombe. Write a letter to Count Fosco at his new home overseas. Tell him what you think about him and what will happen if he returns to England.

39 Write a newspaper report about Sir Percival's death. Say who he was, how he died and give the conclusion of the official enquiry.

40 Discuss this statement: Marian and Laura are very different characters.

41 Write a review of the novel. Briefly describe the story and give your opinion of it.

42 Who you regard as the most evil, Sir Percival or Count Fosco?

43 Discuss this statement: *The Woman in White* is a novel in which the plot is more important than the characters.

44 Explain why Anne Catherick's role in the story is essentially tragic.

45 The story is told from the point of view of a number of characters. Why did Collins choose this way of telling the story and how successful is it?

46 Write a diary entry by Laura written soon after she has gone to live secretly in London with Marian and Walter.

WORD LIST

accomplice (n) a person who helps someone such as a criminal to do something wrong

adjoin (v) to be next to and connected to

affection (n) a feeling of liking or love and caring

ancestor (n) a member of your family who lived a long time ago

angel (n) a spirit who is God's servant in heaven

asylum (n) (an old word for) a mental hospital

confined (adj) not able to move outside a small area

crackling (n) the sound that is made when something burns

exclaim (v) to say something suddenly and loudly because you are surprised, angry, or excited

fascinating (adj) extremely interesting

forgery (n) something, such as a document, that looks genuine but is not

fulfil (v) to achieve or make real

gamekeeper (n) someone whose job is to look after wild animals and birds that are kept to be hunted on private land

gasp (n) a sudden intake of breath which shows surprise or pain

gloomy (adj) dark, especially in a way that makes you feel sad

lantern (n) a lamp that you can carry, consisting of a metal container with glass sides that surrounds a flame or light

maid (n) a female servant, especially in a large house or hotel

marble (n) a type of hard rock that is used in buildings

meantime (n) the period of time between now and a future event

relieved (adj) feeling happy because you are no longer worried about something

restore (v) to return something or someone to a former state or condition

settlement (n) an agreed sum of money that is paid

sigh (v/n) to breathe out making a long sound, to express a feeling such as boredom or disappointment

situated (adj) positioned

sketch (n/v) a quickly-made drawing

veil (n) a thin piece of material that a woman can wear to partly cover her face

veranda (n) an open area with a floor and a roof that is attached to the side of a house at ground level

vestry (n) a small room in a church where a priest puts on his or her special clothes and where holy plates, cups etc are kept

waistcoat (n) a piece of clothing without sleeves that has buttons down the front and is worn over a shirt, often under a jacket as part of a man's suit

The Moonstone
Wilkie Collins

The Moonstone is an ancient Indian diamond which brings disaster to everyone who owns it. Rachel Verinder's uncle gives her the diamond as a birthday present, but that same night it is stolen . . . *The Moonstone* is now seen as the first, and one of the best, English detective novels.

Great Expectations
Charles Dickens

Pip is a poor orphan whose life is changed for ever by two very different meetings – one with an escaped convict and the other with an eccentric old lady and the beautiful girl who lives with her. And who is the mysterious person who leaves him a fortune?

Oliver Twist
Charles Dickens

His mother is dead, so little Oliver Twist is brought up in the workhouse. Beaten and starved, he runs away to London, where he joins Fagin's gang of thieves. By chance he also finds good new friends – but can they protect him from people who rob and murder without mercy?

Crime and Punishment
Fyodor Dostoevsky

Raskolnikoff, a young student, has been forced to give up his university studies because of lack of money. He withdraws from society and, poor and lonely, he develops a plan to murder a greedy old moneylender. Surely the murder of one worthless old woman would be excused, even approved of, if it made possible a thousand good deeds? But this crime is just the beginning of the story. Afterwards he must go on a journey of self-discovery. He must try to understand his motives and explain them to others. Can he succeed?

Les Misérables
Victor Hugo

Jean Valjean is free at last after nineteen years in prison. Cold and hungry, he is rejected by everyone he meets. But Jean's life is changed forever when he discovers love. He spends the rest of his life helping people, like himself, who have been victims of poverty and social injustice – 'les misérables'.

Captain Corelli's Mandolin
Louis de Bernières

Louis de Bernières is one of the best writers in English today.

This is a great love story set in the tragedy of war. It is 1941. The Italian officer, Captain Corelli, falls in love with Pelagia, a young Greek girl. But Pelegia's fiancé is fighting the Italian army . . .

Captain Corelli's Mandolin is now a film, starring Nicholas Cage.

There are hundreds of Penguin Readers to choose from – world classics, film adaptations, modern-day crime and adventure, short stories, biographies, American classics, non-fiction, plays ...

For a complete list of all Penguin Readers titles, please contact your local Pearson Longman office or visit our website.

www.penguinreaders.com